CAKE

Edible

Series Editor: Andrew F. Smith

EDIBLE is a revolutionary new series of books dedicated to food and drink that explores the rich history of cuisine. Each book reveals the global history and culture of one type of food or beverage.

Already published

Caviar Nichola Fletcher

Cheese Andrew Dalby

Chocolate Sarah Moss and Alexander Badenoch

Curry Colleen Taylor Sen

Hamburger Andrew F. Smith

Hot Dog Bruce Kraig

Milk Hannah Velten

Pancake Ken Albala

Pie Janet Clarkson

Pizza Carol Helstosky

Spices Fred Czarra

Forthcoming

Apple Erika Janik

Barbeque Jonathan Deutsch

Beer Bob Skilnik

Bread William Rubel

Champagne Becky Sue Epstein

Cocktails Joseph M. Carlin

Coffee Jonathan Morris

Dates Nawal Nasrallah

Egg Diane Toops

Fish and Chips Panikos Panayi

Gin Lesley Jacobs Solmonson

Herbs Gary Allen

Ice Cream Laura Weiss

Lobster Elisabeth Townsend

Offal Nina Edwards

Olive Fabrizia Lanza

Pasta Kantha Shelke

Porridge Oliver B. Pollak

Potato Andrew F. Smith

Rice Renee Marton

Rum Richard Foss

Sandwich Bee Wilson

Soup Janet Clarkson

Tea Helen Saberi

Tomato Deborah A. Duchon

Vodka Patricia Herlihy

Whiskey Kevin R. Kosar

Wine Marc Millon

Cake

A Global History

Nicola Humble

REAKTION BOOKS

Published by Reaktion Books Ltd
33 Great Sutton Street
London EC1V 0DX, UK
www.reaktionbooks.co.uk

First published 2010

Printed and bound in China by Eurasia

British Library Cataloguing in Publication Data

Humble, Nicola.
Cake : a global history. – (Edible)
1. Cake.
2. Cake – History.
3. Cake in literature.
I. Title II. Series
641.8´653-DC22

ISBN 978 1 86189 648 3

Contents

Introduction:
When is a Cake not a Cake?

The first cake I remember was a train. It had chocolate biscuit wheels, a Cadbury's mini-roll funnel, and windows made of sweets and glacé cherries. It ran on a track of chocolate fingers and angelica. My mum made it, probably from instructions in a magazine – *Women's Weekly* or *Family Circle*. It was my birthday cake the year I was five. I have no memory of what it tasted like, or even of eating it. Birthday cake wasn't really for eating, it was for looking at. I expect my friends were given squares wrapped in paper napkins and that they got squashed in their party bags on the way home. I remember it because it was my cake, made for me. It was a symbol of celebration, of the specialness of being the birthday girl. It was food that was played with, turned into a toy. It was treat piled on treat, so sweet and sickly that no child could manage more than a few bites.

Now a mother myself, I swear each year that I will not go overboard on my son's birthday cake, and each year the construction is more complicated, more ambitious, more absurd. A chest full of treasure for a pirate picnic party (the lid slid off when I tried to move it); a planet complete with marzipan aliens for a space party; a piñata cake with a chocolate bowl over it which the birthday boy cracked with a hammer; a pyramid cake with a secret tomb inside it. I am well aware that I reach the limits of sanity with these constructions – toiling obsessively late into the night. At the parties the guests glance at them briefly and then ignore them. This is cake at the edge of rationality: excessive, outlandish, its form utterly overwhelming its function, its status as food only notional. These cakes are maternal anxiety and culinary ego made solid. My feelings about them are as much shame as pride.

Cakes are very strange things, producing a range of emotional responses far out of keeping with their culinary significance. They are simultaneously utterly unnecessary and absolutely crucial. You can't properly have a birthday or a wedding without a cake. Christmas cake is central to our celebration, yet its inedible hardness is legendary – the family jokes about saws and the cake that will never die part of the point. Cake is one of those foodstuffs whose symbolic function can completely overwhelm its actual status as comestible. More than anything, cake is an idea. But cakes are also incontrovertibly material: lusciously spongy or solid with fruit, sticky, creamy, loaded with sweetness, filled and iced and decorated: food layered on food. They are unmistakeable; ineffably present in their sweet excess.

Yet despite their assertive, insistent materiality, cakes are also curiously fugitive. Start to trace the history of cake and you are soon lost in a thicket of competing definitions. Because there is a central problem: how do we know a cake when we see one? Is a cake a cake because it is round, or because it is flat? Is it because it is soft, or because it is compressed? Is it a cake if it is made light and spongy with eggs or baking agents? Can it still be a cake if the raising agent is yeast? Or does cake-ness instead depend on the structural role the food plays? If it is the sweet centrepiece of a celebration, is it a cake? If it is served with tea in the afternoon, or coffee in the morning, does it qualify? In certain cultures, at certain historical moments, each of these elements has been the crucial one in defining a cake.

Then there are the many border disputes between cake and its near neighbours: how and why does cake differ from bread? When does the boundary between these closely related foods become fixed? And how do we draw the line between cake and a whole host of cousins: tea-bread, biscuits, cookies, muffins, scones, pastries and puddings? Are pancakes cakes? What about cheesecakes? Such questions might seem solely the territory of the food-nerd, yet they have been behind some high-profile court battles in recent years. Most notable is the case of Jaffa Cakes, whose manufacturer, McVitie's, launched a case against the UK Inland Revenue in 1991, arguing that their chocolate-coated orange-centred confections were cakes and not biscuits, and therefore should not be liable for VAT.[1] The company won their case, basing their claim on the culinary principle that the crucial difference between biscuits and cakes is that cakes dry as they stale and biscuits soften. Fair enough; yet three years later, Marks & Spencer mounted a similar case over their chocolate teacakes (a mound of marshmallow on a chocolate biscuit, covered in milk chocolate) which they took all the way to the European Court of Justice. The eventual decision, reached in April 2008 after twelve years of legal wrangling, that the British government should refund £3.5 million of overpaid tax to the company, seems to have been based not on a culinary principle of the difference between cakes and biscuits, but on a peculiarly intuitive sense (which the British government conceded at the very start of the case) that M&S's teacakes, with their round-ness, their squishy filling, their richness, their *name*, were somehow culturally cakes, despite the presence of that base of (whisper it) biscuit. Identifying a cake can be more com-plicated than we think.

I
Cakes through History

Cake has either a very long or a surprisingly short history, depending on how you look at it. Archaeologists have found evidence of foods they call cakes from the very earliest civilizations, and yet the sort of foodstuff Anglo-Americans usually mean by the term (sweet, soft, spongy) only really comes into being in the mid-eighteenth century. The linguistic category that we denote by the name 'cake' does not map neatly onto the food-concepts employed even by our nearest neighbours (the French *gâteaux* or German *Torten* being by no means synonymous), let alone those of more distant neighbours or earlier historical periods. Nonetheless, I will attempt in this chapter, albeit tentatively, to trace the culinary, linguistic and conceptual roots of the modern cake.

Those earliest cakes discovered by archaeologists in the remains of Neolithic lake villages in Switzerland were flat rounds of crushed grain, moistened, compacted and cooked, in all probability, on a hot stone in the ashes of a fire. These are 'cakes' because of their flat, compacted nature (a linguistic usage that survives in the case of a 'cake' of soap). Such cakes are the ancient version of the modern oatcake which, despite its name, we would now put in the category of biscuit or cracker. This definition of cake as something squished

A detail from the Nereid Monument, *c.* 400 BC, showing two figures bearing cakes in a procession.

together into a patty-like form (think also of cattle cakes, or rice cakes) is a dominant one in the food of the classical world. There are a number of food stuffs that classicists commonly translate as cake. The Ancient Greek *plakous*, which becomes the Roman *placenta*, is a form of flat cake that appears in many texts, though with what seems to be considerable variation in its ingredients. The Roman sources also commonly name *libum*, which is usually a form of cheesecake, often covered in honey. Cakes appear most often in religious contexts: the Egyptian Greek Athenaeus, writing about AD 200, lists a number, including the *amphiphon*, a flat cake surrounded by small torches which was used in offerings to Artemis and Hecate; the *basynias*, a boiled wheat dough filled with honey, walnuts and dried figs, which the Delians sacrificed to Iris; and the *mulloi*, made from sesame and honey in the shape of a woman's genital organs, carried in Syracuse in processions for Demeter and Persephone.[1] Most of these cakes seem likely to have evolved from 'poured' religious offerings of grain, milk, nuts and honey, with the Greek terms *pelanos* and *popanon* signifying both the poured and the cake-like concepts. In the second century BC, the Roman senator Cato the Elder lists a considerable quantity of different types of cake in his *On Agriculture*, a fact which has tended to surprise editors of this otherwise austere writer, but which suggests that the concept of cake was of some importance in the classical world, and that it denoted a wide variety of very different food stuffs with very different social and culinary functions: 'Cakes covered so wide a range of eating in antiquity that the same name might be applied to a rustic confection as a rich man's titbit, and the same name to "luxurious" Persian desserts as to a religious offering.'[2]

The compacted form of cake has a long history, surviving in Britain into the medieval period in the form of ginger-

A Corinthian terracotta figure of a mule bears a load which includes cakes, 350 BC.

'The Gingerbread Makers', engraving by Jan Luyken, *c.* 1742.

bread, which was usually made by mixing breadcrumbs to
a stiff paste with honey and spices such as pepper, saffron,
cinnamon and ginger, and then shaped by pressing it into
a square. Because of the high cost of spices this was an
expensive sweetmeat. It was often decorated: early versions
have box leaves attached with the sharp points of cloves,
arranged in a pattern to resemble the studding on tooled
leather armour, with the leaves forming a heraldic fleur-de-
lis and the cloves driven in like nails.[3] Gingerbread in this
form continued into the seventeenth century, when red

gingerbread was popular, flavoured with cinnamon, aniseed and ginger and coloured with liquorice and red wine. It was rolled out thin, pressed with a decorated mould to print a picture on its surface, and then dried in the oven.[4] Much gingerbread was imported from the Netherlands, and it is notable that such wooden moulds continue to this day to be used by Dutch cooks to print shortbread-type biscuits.

The ancient compressed cake serves much the same structural function as the modern cake: a centrepiece to celebrations and feast days. We might even draw comparisons between the ancient use of cake as a compound religious offering – good, luxurious things crammed together – and the later function of cake as a symbolic offering at celebrations of birthdays or weddings. But in evolutionary terms the compressed cake is a blind alley. Modern cakes do not descend from it. Indeed, it is as modern baking techniques begin to emerge in the seventeenth century that the old form of gingerbread dies out, being replaced by a version involving flour, butter, sugar and eggs as well as the spices of the original.[5]

So from what does the modern cake evolve? Its most obvious ancestor is bread, and for much of their history bread and cake were virtually indistinguishable:

> The evidence for early forms of cake in Britain is elusive. In any case the boundary between primitive bread and primitive cake was tenuous, honey- and milk-breads being made when the extra ingredients were available. If fat was also added, to be taken up as the starch granules of the flour swelled and burst during cooking, the result might be a kind of cake.[6]

Cake does not become firmly separated from bread for a very long time. Even the linguistic derivation of the word

Elijah being fed cakes and wine by an angel, from a 13th-century biblical manuscript.

'cake' is uncertain, with some sources assuming it derives from the Old Norse 'kaka' and others claiming it as a Latin loan word via Ancient British or Anglo-Saxon. The first written evidence dates from the 1300s. The term cake, when used, seems to refer most specifically to forms of bread that are enriched and flat, with flatness being the key distinguishing characteristic. One early definition of cake is given by John de Trevisa in 1398, where the crucial feature distinguishing cake from bread seems to be that it is turned over during baking and is therefore flat on both sides: 'Some brede is bake and tornyd and wende at fyre and is callyd . . . a cake.'[7] The cake mentioned in the Prologue of Chaucer's *Canterbury Tales* is both flat and round: it is carried by the drunken Summoner, who is comically using it in lieu of a shield: 'A bokeleer hadde he maade hym of a cake.'[8] Cakes in the Middle Ages could be both large and small: in medieval English word lists 'cake' is usually glossed with the Latin *pastillus*, meaning a little cake or pie, but in the Reeve's tale Chaucer describes a cake which takes half a bushel (13 kg) of flour. Such large cakes, flavoured with spices and sugar or honey, raised with ale barm, and enriched with cream, butter and eggs were served as centrepieces at grand occasions. Small cakes of enriched bread – buns to us today – were a much more familiar foodstuff during the Middle Ages and beyond. These are the cakes of Sir Toby Belch's ringing retort to the parsimonious steward Malvolio in *Twelfth Night*: 'Dost thou think because thou art virtuous, there shall be no more cakes and ale?'[9] Cakes here stand for pleasure; they belong to a category of entertainment – like plays, circuses and recreational sex – that the Puritans are seeking to outlaw. Indeed, in 1592, ten years before Shakespeare's play was first performed, the Lord Clerk of the Markets issued a decree forbidding bakers 'at any time or times hereafter [to] make, utter, or sell by retail, within or without their houses, unto any of the Queen's subjects any spice cakes, buns, biscuits, or other spice bread'; the only occasions excepted from this rule were funerals, Christmas and Good Friday. The cross-topped, spiced, fruited bun we still eat on the latter day survives virtually unchanged from its Tudor form.[10] In the time of James I there were further attempts to prevent bakers from making spice breads and buns, but these proved impossible to reinforce, and a wide range of local variations of these enriched cake-breads continued to be made for centuries. These include the now-extinct wigs – lightly spiced buns which were eaten with a drink of chocolate by fashionable breakfasters in the seventeenth century – Chelsea buns, Bath buns, Cornish splits, the rarer Sussex plum heavies, and larger cakes such as Bath's famous Sally Lunn, Northumberland lardy cake and Cornish saffron cake.

Today, our culinary taxonomy would assign such food to the category of sweet bread rather than cake, despite the fact that some of them retain the name 'cake'. It is notable that virtually all modern recipes for delicacies like the immensely rich lardy cake (in which the dough is interleaved with cubes of lard and brown sugar) are prefaced with an explanation that it is really a form of bread. The ramshackle, piecemeal, random processes of culinary evolution mean that many foodstuffs remain stranded on the wrong side of the in-any-case very shaky line dividing bread from cake in the British imagination. Take, for instance, the case of teacakes and tea-breads. Each derives its name from the meal at which it is commonly served rather than because tea is an ingredient. Teacakes, which we most often encounter in teashops in small tourist towns and villages, are fruited yeast-raised buns, served split, toasted and buttered at afternoon tea. They belong to the class of small breads that includes muffins and crumpets, and are cakes only in the sense that they are flat and round. Tea-breads, confusingly, *are* cakes. Raised with chemical agents such as bicarbonate of soda, these are light, relatively plain cakes, which would usually be served at high tea – that curious meal which survives from the rural traditions of the late nineteenth and early twentieth centuries, and which traditionally includes bread and butter, a simple protein dish such as boiled eggs, ham or kippers, and a fairly plain cake. Tea-breads are bread because of their shape – they are cooked in loaf tins, sliced like bread, and often served buttered.

Despite such fascinating anomalies, it is broadly true to say that for the modern British, yeast-raised goods fall outside the conventional category of cake. This is by no means the case for other European nations. Many of the most famous cakes of countries such as France, Germany, Austria and Italy are yeast-raised. The kugelhopf or gugelhopf, baked in a tall, round, decorative mould with a hole in the centre, is a speciality in Alsace, Austria, Germany and Poland, where it may well have originated in the early 1600s. The French savarin and its close relative the rum baba are based on a rich brioche-type yeasted dough, their compact, soft and squashy texture deriving from the alcoholic syrup with which they are soaked. Germany's brandy-drenched, marzipan-stuffed Christmas stollen; Italy's towering vanilla-scented panettone: all fall into a conceptual category much closer to cake than bread. Dishes such as these, transplanted across the Atlantic by Dutch, German and Scandinavian settlers, evolved into the category known to Americans as coffee cakes. Yeast-raised doughs, often in ring form and variously covered with streusel toppings, drizzled with nuts, honey or syrups, or filled with custard or cream cheese, these are served mid-morning with coffee: an elaboration of an earlier tradition of sweet bread as a breakfast food.

Toasted teacakes in a Cambridge tea-shop.

Our modern cake has other ancestors besides bread. One is an even more primitive food than bread: porridge. Early man is thought to have rendered hard grains edible by soaking and boiling them into a sort of porridge. By the Middle Ages, porridge existed in many forms, one of which was an enriched version in which the oats or wheat were accompanied by dried fruits, suet, butter, honey and spices. This luxurious mixture had a celebratory function, and was often served at Christmas. This 'plum porridge' ('plum' being the generic medieval term for dried fruits) eventually became so stiff with ingredients that it was more solid than liquid. It was at this stage that cooks began to boil it in a cloth, developing the glossy, round plum pudding that was later to play so central a role in the Victorian Christmas. The same mixture could also be baked, with ale barm added to raise it: the derivation of these early rich fruit cakes from the pudding is indicated by their commonest name – 'plum pudding cake'. The fruit cake was much rarer than the pudding because of the relative rarity of bread ovens throughout the medieval period. Because of the fire risk they posed, only large manors and monasteries had ovens, housed in separate bakehouses away from the main buildings. It was only in the sixteenth century that the walls of cottages began to be sturdy enough to safely incorporate an oven: before that, most baking was done on the open hearthstones. One result of this was to restrict the 'great' (or large) cake to the inhabitants of great houses – and even then, the expense of their ingredients made them strictly feast-day foods. The fruit cake that derives from porridge via pudding is not ultimately separable from the fruit cake that is an enriched form of bread, though the proportion of fruit to other ingredients in the former would tend to be higher, and the texture of the cake therefore denser. The more one looks into the history of food, the clearer it becomes that most foodstuffs have a number of different ancestors and several parallel strands of development. Dishes emerge almost always through a process of accident and serendipity rather than out of reasoned 'scientific' development.

Another precursor of the modern cake is the pancake. The ancient batter of eggs, milk and flour, particularly when fried in a shallow pan rather than on a griddle, is not so different from later raised batter cakes. The crucial distinction is in the use of the eggs. It took a surprisingly long time for the raising power of beaten egg whites to be discovered. The earliest sources we have are from the cooks of the Italian Renaissance. The dating of these sources does not, of course, give us the moment of the discovery of beaten egg white. It invariably takes a long time for advances in cooking technique to be recorded in written form – often as much as a generation. We do know that dishes involving the beating of egg whites were already a feature at the Elizabethan court, particularly 'snow', a dish of egg whites beaten with cream, which in its earliest form is a feast dish for Christmas, mounded over an apple and decorated with a 'bush' of rosemary. The whisking of egg whites was of considerable technical difficulty before the invention of the fork – early cooks accomplished it through the use of devices such as bound bunches of peeled twigs or by squeezing the whites repeatedly through a sponge. Beaten egg whites, or eggs beaten whole, were soon found to be sufficient to raise the smaller forms of baked goods. The earliest recipe published in English for what is essentially a modern sponge cake is given by Gervase Markham in *The English Huswife* of 1615:

> To make Bisket-bread, take a pound of fine flower, and a pound of Sugar finely beaten and searsed, and mix them

The earliest-known image of an egg whisk, which is wielded by an apprentice in a kitchen scene from Bartolomeo Scappi's *Opera* (1570).

together, then take eight eggs, & put four yelks, and beat them together, then strew in your flower & sugar as you are beating of it, by a little at once, it will take very near an hours beating: then take half an ounce of Anniseeds and

Coriander seeds, and let them be dryed and rubb'd very clean, and put them in: then rub your Bisket-pans with cold sweet butter as thin as you can, and so put it in, and bake it in an Oven: but if you would have thin Cakes, then take fruit-dishes, and rub them in like sort with butter, and so bake your Cakes on them, and when they are almost baked, turn them, and thrust them down close with your hand. Some to this Biskuit-bread will add a little Cream, and it is not amiss, but excellent good also.[11]

There are many interesting features of this recipe which makes it worth quoting in full. The cake is designated as 'biscuit bread' when it is large, and as 'cake' only when it is small and pressed flat after baking (and so much more like a modern biscuit or cookie). The extraordinary length of time required to beat the mixture is notable, as is the fact that the flour is beaten with the eggs and sugar, rather than added gently at the end, as in modern cake baking. The effect would be to lengthen the strings of gluten in the flour to some extent – producing a rather chewy cake. Also significant is the addition of seeds – a feature in virtually all non-fruited British cake until well into the nineteenth century.

Slowly, throughout the seventeenth and eighteenth centuries, the 'modern' cake began to emerge. It could not have come into being without the development of a number of new culinary technologies. The first was the cake hoop, a precursor of the cake pan, which came into use towards the end of the seventeenth century. It could be made of wood, tin or paper, and, placed on a flat baking tray, allowed for the construction of cakes in the form of flattish straight-sided cylinders, rather than the shallow dome shape of an unsupported cake. The use of the hoop had an effect on the texture of the cake, reducing the formation of a crust at the sides. The development of ovens also contributed to the evolution of the cake. Cupboards with iron doors were built into chimney walls close to the fire to provide small baking ovens in which bread, cakes and pies could be cooked. The invention of the kitchen range in 1780 allowed for the control of baking temperature and made possible lighter and more delicate cakes.

The most significant change was the one that separated the British cake decisively from bread – the removal of yeast as a raising agent. This change happened so gradually that it is hard to pinpoint the exact moment of transition. Robert Smith's *Court Cookery* of 1725 has recipes only for yeast-raised cakes, while just two years later Elizabeth Smith's *The Compleat Housewife* has several cakes raised entirely with eggs, including 'a rich Great Cake' and 'a good Seed Cake'. It would be tempting, then, to date the emergence of the egg-raised cake to 1727, but cookbooks are, as I have noted, a very inexact guide to culinary practices. The most we can conclude is that it was in the early years of the eighteenth century that it began to be clear to cooks that a cake with sufficient eggs did not also require ale barm to raise it. The two forms of cake exist side-by-side in cookery books throughout the eighteenth and into the nineteenth century, with a solitary yeast-raised cake to be found as late as 1861 in Isabella Beeton's *Book of Household Management*. Yeast tends, increasingly, to be reserved as a raising method for the plainer cheaper cakes; Beeton's cake is designated 'Common Cake, suitable for sending to Children at School'.

It took a lot of eggs to replace the raising power of yeast. The commonest form of the new cake was a pound cake, so called because the recipe required a pound each of butter, sugar and flour, and roughly the equivalent weight in eggs (usually eight). This ratio provided sufficient raising power to leaven even cakes rich in fruit. All such recipes required a lengthy beating of the eggs, with some beating yolks and whites separately and some together. These cakes were an arduous undertaking – directions not uncommonly suggest at least an hour's beating to cream together the butter and sugar, and then allow the same time again for the whisking of the eggs. The caricature image of the enormously muscled cook has its basis in physical reality.

The final stage in the evolution of the modern cake was the development of chemical raising agents. The first was 'pearl ash'– potassium carbonate prepared from wood ash – which was used in America from the 1790s. The mildly alkaline substance formed bubbles when mixed with a mild acid such as sour milk; the reaction is instant, unlike that of yeast, allowing for the production of quick 'breads' and cakes. The problem with pearl ash was that it reacted with fats to produce a pronounced soapy flavour. It was later replaced by bicarbonate of soda, which, although it reacted similarly, did so much less strongly. Around 1850 'true' baking powder was invented – in which an acid (usually cream of tartar) and an alkali (bicarbonate of soda) were already combined. A small amount of starch was added to dispel moisture, which would have caused the chemical reaction to start prematurely. Baking powder allowed for the development of soft, light, spongy cakes without the necessity of a large proportion of eggs and lengthy whisking. The modern cake had arrived.

The Icing on the Cake

If a great cake was intended for a particularly important occasion it might be iced. The earliest form of icing involved painting a cake hot from the oven with egg whites beaten with rosewater, sprinkling it with sugar and returning it to a low oven to dry. The ideal, according to Sir Kenelm Digby, writing in 1669, should look 'pure, white and smooth like silver between polished and matte or like a looking glass'.[12] What the cook had to avoid was scorching the icing, presumably a common fault, since so many cookbooks warn against it. The quantity of sugar involved in icing a cake increased throughout the seventeenth and eighteenth centuries, and the sugar began to be beaten together with the other ingredients before being applied to the cake: Hannah Glasse advises that the icing should be spread over the cake with 'a Brush or Bundle of Feathers'.[13] Sugar was already 'double-refined' in English refineries by the early seventeenth century, but it still represented a major expenditure of effort to cut sections from the rock-hard cone and reduce it to a fine powder in a mortar. Before sugar was used for icing, it was put to much more spectacular use, in the 'subtleties' or 'sotelties' of the medieval court. Constructed of spiced sugar paste, almond paste and quince jelly, these were elaborate sculptures depicting landscapes and castles, decorated with people and animals. Their function was primarily to be a spectacle – they were displayed between the courses of the grandest of feasts. When these constructions went out of fashion during the sixteenth century the almond paste remained in the form of marchpane, which was served in a large round cake, often iced, as part of the final sweet course of a feast. The marzipan was revived as a layer between cake and icing in the late eighteenth century. As well as tasting good, it enhanced keeping qualities by separating the moist cake from the dry icing. It also meant that the icing itself no longer needed to go into the oven as it could be made to melt to a glassy sheet through contact with the hot

Italian bakers decorating giant cakes in the style of English birthday cakes in an early 20th-century illustration by Italian artist Achille Beltrame.

marzipan. Sugar production was mechanized at about the same time, which allowed for the production of very finely powdered sugar, also known as confectioner's or icing sugar. Since the sugar was so fine, it was no longer necessary to melt it to achieve a smooth, glassy icing. Modern royal icing, the 'traditional' covering for wedding or Christmas cakes, uses the same ingredients as the earliest icing and dries to a rock-hard finish. Less elaborate forms of icing, such as water ice or boiled icing, use just icing sugar and water (sometimes milk), simply mixed, in the case of the former, or boiled to a thick paste. These icings form a slightly dry crust but remain soft underneath and are commonly used on soft cakes such as Victoria Sandwiches or cupcakes. American frostings of the 'seven minute' varieties use similar ingredients to royal icing, but employ a method that yields very different results. Eggs and powdered sugar are whisked together over heat for the specified seven minutes to form a type of sugar-dense meringue. The texture remains soft – somewhere between marshmallow and meringue – and the icing is piled onto the cake in exuberant swirls and whorls, the opposite of the scrupulously flat restrained surface of royal icing: clichés of national personality rendered in sugar. If a French cake is iced it will usually be with either a chocolate ganache (cream and chocolate melted together) or a fondant icing, made by thinning fondant (a creamy textured preparation of sugar and glucose syrup boiled to the soft-ball stage, kneaded and left to ripen) with water and pouring it over the cake. The fondant dries to a firm glossy finish but is soft to the bite, allowing for the creation of elegant yet palatable morsels.

The modern cake is as likely to be covered in buttercream as it is in conventional icing. It seems to have been in Germany that buttercream filling was first developed, at the end of the nineteenth century.[14] It is probable that it was invented by chefs looking for an alternative to cream, the quality and consistency of which had been altered by new laws of pasteurization. Buttercream was also malleable in a way whipped cream was not, and this fact, along with the

A British display of elaborate cakes, chromolithograph, 1874.

technological development of fine pressed tin piping nozzles, opened up a whole new set of decorative possibilities. The cartoon sculptures which have been popular for children's birthday cakes since the 1970s were at first covered in butter-cream, and more recently in a 'plastic' sugar-paste icing that can be tinted in bright colours, rolled out and stretched over the cake to produce a smooth and professional-looking surface.

2

Cakes around the World

Visiting Naples in the late 1930s, Jean-Paul Sartre eyed up the men, 'decked in white linen, gleaming teeth, and sparkling but weary eyes'. Finding them glassily resistant to his gaze, he turned his attention instead to the cakes in the elegant patisseries of the city's Via Roma:

> Cakes are human, they are like faces. Spanish cakes are ascetic with a swaggering appearance, they crumble into dust under the tooth. Greek cakes are greasy like little oil lamps: when you press them, the oil oozes out. German cakes are bulky and soft like shaving cream; they are made so that obese easily tempted men can eat them indulgently, without worrying what they taste like but simply to fill their mouths with sweetness. But those Italian cakes had a cruel perfection: really small and flawless, scarcely bigger than petits fours, they gleamed. Their harsh and gaudy colours took away any desire to eat them; instead, you felt like placing them on the side-board like pieces of painted porcelain.[1]

For Sartre cakes speak parodically of the clichés of national identity: they separate. But it is not so easy in practice to

Women at a Café, 1924, oil on canvas by Italian painter Piero Marussig.

isolate the cakes of different nations: the history of the development of the modern cake is one of synergies as well as separations. Evolved out of the very varied culinary traditions of many European nations, cake figures unity even in its differences.

One key strand in its history begins in Italy, with the chefs of the Italian Renaissance, most famously Bartolomeo Scappi, who cooked for cardinals and popes in the mid-sixteenth century, and was among the first European cooks to borrow from the pastry-making traditions of the Arab world. It is in Scappi's *Opera* of 1570 that we find the earliest references to key techniques in the making of sponge cakes: as well as depicting the whisking of egg whites he also, in a recipe for '*zambaglione*', describes the process of whisking whole eggs and sugar together over heat. These techniques spread across Europe, with German chef Marx Rumpolt giving a recipe for 'Pisctoten von lauter Eyerweiss' (biscuits made only with egg whites) in his *Ein new Kochbuch* of 1581. Half a century later, the centre of culinary advance had shifted to France, where court chefs developed a cuisine that decisively broke with the tastes and habits of the Middle Ages. La Varenne, author of *Le Cuisinier françois* of 1651, the first cookbook to lay out these new developments, was also credited with the authorship of a book specifically concerned with patisserie. *Le Pâtissier françois*, which first appeared anonymously in 1653, is a remarkably detailed work, offering step-by-step instructions and detailed measurements and temperatures. The methods for making puff pastry, macaroons and waffles are pretty much identical to those of today. It is the first work to mention the small ovens called *petits fours*, which were to give their name to that distinctively French group of miniature decorated cakes.[2]

The elaborate tradition of French patisserie reached its apotheosis in the hands of Antonin (Marie-Antoine) Carême. Born in 1784, five years before the beginning of the French Revolution, Carême was abandoned at the age of ten by his very poor family, and left to make his own living. He was taken in by a cookshop, where he served an apprenticeship for seven years, before finding work as a confectioner in the fashionable patisserie of Bailly. From there he moved to the grand kitchens of the Prince de Talleyrand, one of the most famous statesmen of the day. Although employed as a pastry cook, Carême contrived to also study general cookery under the chef Boucher. By the time he left, he had already surpassed the skills of his master. Carême became the most famous chef of his day, employed by a startling number of eminent international patrons, including the Prince Regent,

Czar Alexander I, the Austrian court, and M. de Rothschild. In the field of culinary history, Carême is renowned for his codification, in a series of books, of the methods and practices of what was to become 'classic' French cookery. But he was always also a patissier, and much of his intellectual energy was given to the creation and recording of elaborate architectural confections. 'The fine arts', he famously insisted, 'are five in number – painting, sculpture, poetry, music,

A design for a *pièce montée* of a 'Pavillion Italien' in Marie-Antoine Carême's *Le Pâtissier Pittoresque* (1842).

Pavillon Italien.

architecture – whose main branch is confectionery.' The pastry cook in a great French kitchen was responsible for preparing the *pièces montées*, the elaborate decorative centre-pieces of the meal. Such grand confections had been popular in the Middle Ages, but they reached their high point in the France of the eighteenth and nineteenth centuries. Carême published two books on patisserie, *Le Pâtissier royal parisien* and *Le Pâtissier pittoresque* (both 1815), which concentrate almost exclusively on these astoundingly elaborate constructions. He specialized particularly in buildings, giving designs for ruins, temples, pavilions and castles. The current edition of the *Larousse Gastronomique*, the bible of French cooking, lists a series of designs, descending from Carême, of 'classic' forms for the *pièce montée*: 'the harp, the lyre, the globe, the Chinese pagoda, the horn of plenty, the ship, the chapel, the bandstand, the waterfall, the Louis xv carriage, the dolphin on the rock, the harvester's basket, the temple and the cart.'[3] Such confections were not necessarily edible, though those of Carême's day usually were, at least in principle. Their basis was not always cake, but cake and associated substances, such as biscuits, marzipan, creams and icings, were the most usual components of their construction. More importantly for a history of cake, the *pièce montée* contributed significantly to the tradition of the elaborately decorated cake as symbolic centrepiece for feasts and celebrations. Other nineteenth-century chefs also specialized in these constructions. Urbain Dubois, a follower of Carême, and at one time chef to the King of Prussia, produced even more elaborate artifices than those of his master, including inedible articles in the constructions. In Britain, Alexis Soyer, the most famous chef of his day, was known for equally elaborate extravaganzas. Soyer, the chef at the Reform Club in the 1840s, was seldom out of the papers. Whether he was

An elaborate boat sculpted in cake and biscuits, Georgia, *c.* 1888–1900.

setting up portable soup kitchens of his own design in Dublin at the height of the Irish potato famine, travelling to the Crimea to re-order the food provision to the British troops, or designing a suit of clothes that could be removed by pulling a string, Soyer was always news. Among his many endeavours, he found the time to write a series of cookery books designed for every level of the market. For the growing urban middle classes there was *The Modern Housewife* (1850), written in the form of letters exchanged between two women; for the poor there was *A Shilling Cookery for the People* (1854); and for the wealthy there was *The Gastronomic Regenerator* (1846), in which he proposes to set out 'a simplified and strikingly new system of cookery'. In fact, the system was basically derived from that of Carême, though somewhat adapted to suit British tastes. The book contains descriptions, couched in Soyer's typically flamboyant and self-regarding prose, of some of the elaborate centrepieces he has prepared for banquets for the rich and famous: a *Hure de Sanglier glacé en surprise* (mock boar's head ice-cream cake), for example, or a *Gâteau Britannique á l'Amiral* (British admiral's cake), in which a sponge cake taking twenty eggs is baked in the form of a ship, with icings, pastes, jellies, wafers, marmalade and jam used to form guns and wood, waves and sails, the whole topped off with rigging made from spun sugar.

As well as such extravagances, the great chefs of the eighteenth and nineteenth centuries developed what might be called a grammar of French baking. The shape, fillings, flavourings and decorations of a whole range of cakes were established in the forms in which they remain to this day. New inventions get added to the repertoire, but each cake has its rules, and free and random innovation is discouraged. So *gâteau Saint Honoré*, a ring of choux pastry piped on top of a base of shortcrust pastry, with caramel-glazed choux buns affixed to the ring, is filled with *crème chiboust* (named for the nineteenth-century pastry cook who invented the *gâteaux*), a custardy pastry-cream thickened with gelatine and lightened with whisked egg whites; while its rival in Parisian patisseries, *gâteau Paris-Brest* (named for the cycle race and designed to imitate the form of a bicycle wheel), also a round of choux pastry, though this time topped with almonds, is split

Nineteenth-century moulded cakes.

and filled with a praline-flavoured cream. When an enterprising pastry-cook decided to fill a *Paris-Brest* with the cream from *Saint Honoré* the resultant cake had to have a new name assigned – *gâteau Paris-Nice*. This is the antithesis of American baking culture, in which each home cook develops her own specialities, tweaking recipes and adding secret ingredients to

LE MARCHAND D'ÉCHAUDÉS

Lebel pinxit.   Joullain Sculpsit.

Amants. pour regaler vos belles   On ne peut flechir les Cruelles
Je suis le Marchand fait exprès,   A moins de soins et moins de frais.
                                                                            Lepine.

a Paris chez Basset & Joullain Quay de la Megisserie a la Ville de Rome Avec Privilege du Roy

An aristocratic couple buy cakes in a French park, etching and engraving by François Joullain, 1760.

make them her own. The French culinary system prizes tradition and exactitude rather than originality and change. French patisserie is essentially a professional matter. The French have little tradition of home baking, and, as Elizabeth David noted, 'it is no disgrace in France – rather the reverse – to say that you have ordered your *gâteau* or *tarte aux fraises* or *savarin aux fruits* from *chez* this or that celebrated *pâtissier*.'[4]

Another major cake tradition is that of what became in the nineteenth century the Austro-Hungarian empire: Austria, and the surrounding lands of Hungary, Bohemia (now part of the Czech Republic), and Moravia (now the Slovak Republic). These nations had a rocky history, with the Austrian Habsburg dynasty annexing and re-annexing its neighbours for centuries. Although there are distinct national traditions, the food cultures of the various nations entwined, in particular in the shared prominence given to desserts, which assume a structural importance unknown in any other European culture. Cakes and pastries are not simply snacks or afterthoughts: they are solidly positioned as food in the cultural practices of these nations, which for centuries have revolved around the institution of the coffee house:

> An Austro-Hungarian café is living history . . . It was from the Café Dommayer that the lilting music of Strauss, inseparable from central European culture, first caressed Viennese ears. The violent 1848 Revolution erupted from Budapest's Café Pilvax. The compeers of Václav Havel and his compatriots organized Czechoslovakia's Velvet Revolution over coffee at the Café Slavia. The intelligentsia of all three cities used the cafés as their living rooms, occasionally laying down their pens to argue the latest developments in literary, art and music circles.[5]

The cakes of France and of the old Austro-Hungary have in common their richness and their ephemerality. Both the *gâteau* and the *torte* are elaborate confections of soft and delicate layers and rich creams, lasting only a single day, designed to be consumed within a few hours of construction. But while the most typical filling in a French cake is pastry cream (a flour-thickened flavoured custard), the pre-eminent central European filling is cream. Whipped cream – *Schlagsahne* to the rest of the German-speaking world, but *Schlagobers* (or, 'very well whipped') to the Viennese – serves many functions in *Kaffee* culture. It is spooned on top of coffee or hot chocolate, and those cakes it doesn't fill it tends to accompany on the plate. So cakes like the famous *Sachertorte*, which often seems disappointingly dry to a non-Austrian palate, need to be understood in the context of the dollop of whipped cream that traditionally sits beside them, and into which each bite of cake is to be dipped.

The differences in form between the cakes of particular culinary traditions is to some extent explained by the meal function they serve. The typically rich, luscious cakes of the Austrian and French traditions sit best with the coffee or tea they are designed to accompany. The tendency of many Italian cakes to be dry and light is accounted for by the fact that they are very often served as an accompaniment to wine. Another class of Italian cakes is just the opposite – positively damp in comparison with the cakes of other European nations. Usually employing ground nuts rather than flour, and often also further dampened with juice or syrup, these are pudding cakes – served at the end of a meal rather than as a snack in their own right. Similar cakes are found in Spain and Portugal. It is possible that these cakes derive originally from the Middle East, where ground nuts are frequently used in cooking of all sorts. One linking factor between these

КОНД.·Ф-КА·"БОЛЬШЕВИК"·МОСКВА

A Russian cake served with a glass of tea.

various cakes is Jewish culinary tradition. Orange and almond cakes are a notable feature of Sephardic culinary tradition (the Sephardi is the branch of the Jewish diaspora whose roots are around Spain, the Mediterranean and the Middle East, as opposed to the Ashkenazi branch of the north). Cakes prepared particularly for Passover replaced flour with ground almonds, while citrus, as Claudia Roden notes, was a feature of Jewish cuisine even when surrounding communities did not make use of it, as the fruit was required for particular religious rituals.[6] One notable version involves whole oranges which are boiled and then minced, pith, rind and all, before being mixed with sugar, whisked whole eggs and ground almonds, to produce a dense, moist cake with the intense orange-ness of marmalade. Germanic culinary culture also makes much use of nuts and seeds in cakes, with darker varieties such as walnuts and poppy seeds being particularly favoured. Unlike British nut and seed cakes, where these ingredients are stirred rather sparsely into a pound-cake base, German cakes use nuts and seeds as a fundamental part of the cake or its filling, replacing the flour in whole or part.

The cultures that have most in common with the British tradition of home baking are the Scandinavian and the Ameri-

Making strudel in a German kitchen, chromolithograph, 1870.

can. Baking plays a very important part in Scandinavian food culture. Until the twentieth century over ninety per cent of the population of the Scandinavian nations lived in scattered, widely dispersed farming communities. Shops were rare, and most food had to be prepared at home. The tradition was that a girl needed to have mastered seven different cakes or cookies before she was ready to marry. Scandinavian baked goods tend to the simple and wholesome, with few, but excellent, ingredients. Where cakes and pastries are complicated it is as the result of craft (very much a feature of Scandinavian culture) rather than because of rich or exotic flavourings. Scandinavian domestic baking is characterized by the use of lots of special tools – patterned rolling pins, tins, irons and moulds – and manual dexterity to create intricate effects. The 'coffee-cake' culture of these nations, in which morning coffee is accompanied by sweet bread or cake, was exported to America by the Finns, Swedes and Norwegians who settled the Midwest in the nineteenth century. There it met up with the baking cultures introduced by many other immigrant groups – Jewish, Italian, German and British, among others – to produce a nation in which baking has a rich and complex set of practices and significances. Aspects of American baking culture will be considered later, but it is worth remarking on one key feature here: the immense hybridity of the influences on American baking leads to some striking regional variations, but the vastness of the landscape and the isolation of rural communities throughout the eighteenth and nineteenth centuries means that home, rather than professional, baking retains a major social significance – if only as an idea.

The cake 'proper' evolved in Europe, and where it has spread around the world it has done so largely as a result of colonialism. South Africa has a significant cake culture which it derives particularly from the Dutch and German settlers who began to arrive in the mid-seventeenth century. They soon discovered highly fertile land which allowed them to establish an excellent wheat crop, and led to the development of a strong tradition of baking. Of particular note is *mosbol-letjie*, a bun leavened with fermented grade juice derived from the wine trade (Laurens van der Post remembers the sight of the buns coming out of the oven 'joined shoulder to shoulder like a battalion of guardsmen trooping the colour, their heads covered in deep dark brown like that of Attic honey').[7] Cakes in Latin America owe much to the influence of Spanish and Portuguese culture. One notable speciality, which is popular throughout Nicaragua, Mexico, Cuba, Puerto Rico and Guatemala, is *Tres Leches* cake, also known as Three Milk Cake. This moist sponge cake is soaked after baking with a mixture of three milk products: evaporated milk, sweetened condensed milk and cream. It is then topped with a layer of vanilla-flavoured whipped cream. There is some dispute about the origins of the cake but it seems probable that it was first disseminated on the back of a can of processed milk. Condensed and evaporated milk are a significant part of Latin American food culture, with dulce de leche, a toffee formed by boiling condensed milk in its can, a much-used ingredient. (In Graham Greene's *The Honorary Consul* of 1973, set in Argentina, a character is said to be 'growing more and more stout on her daily diet of cream-cakes and *alfajores* stuffed with dulce de leche').

One reason that the European cake is not a truly global phenomenon has to do with cooking techniques. There are many nations for whom baking in an enclosed oven is not a part of their culinary repertoire. The Chinese, for instance, do not traditionally have domestic ovens, and their cakes are steamed, producing a very different finished product

Russian-style cakes in a marketplace, Lvov, Ukraine.

(a typical example is Sticky Cake, formed of glutinous rice flour, brown candy, dates and sesame seeds, and cooked by custom at the Spring Festival to appease the Kitchen God, who has to make an annual report to heaven of the family's behaviour over the year). The absence of a culture of domestic baking is also the case in much of Africa, where cakes appear predominantly as street food: coconut 'biscuits' in West and Central Africa, and fried delicacies such as *chin-chin* (crisp fragments of sweet dough), puff-puff and *mandazi* (varieties of doughnut or fritter from, respectively, Nigeria and Kenya). In Japan, as in China, traditional cakes have very little in common with the European model, usually being sweetmeats composed of bean-derived products such as *yōken*, a compressed sweet bean jelly, or *manjū*, a pastry of flour, rice flour and buckwheat wrapped around fillings of azuki bean paste and boiled. But in the period since the Second World War, the Japanese have consumed ever-increasing quantities of Western-style cakes, with light sponge confections topped with whipped cream and strawberries being particularly popular.[8]

Famous Cakes

If the modern cake has found new forms and functions as it has travelled around the globe, it has also accrued layers of narrative and symbolism. Cakes repeatedly become objects of folklore; they get famous, inspiring legends and lawsuits, and squabbles about recipes and origins. The list of famous cakes is vast: *Dobostorte*, *Sachertorte*, Black Forest Gateau, Dundee Cake, Lamingtons, Election Cake, Angel Food Cake, New Orleans King Cakes, Moravian Sugar Cakes, Devil's Food Cake, to name but a few. Some, like the British Twelfth

Cake, no longer exist. Others, like brownies, and the Latin-American *Tres Leches* cake, are recent inventions, the product of recipes dreamed up by the manufacturers of commercial food products. The history of such cakes is often as much a matter of rumour as of fact, with stories elaborated for the benefit of local tourist trades and to enhance the fame of hotels, restaurants and shops. Cakes seem disproportionately to be the subject of such history-construction compared to other foodstuffs. It is interesting to speculate why this might be: perhaps because cakes are portable, and therefore appropriate to sell to tourists as mementos; perhaps because they serve a number of meal functions, appearing variously as part of morning coffee, afternoon tea or coffee, as a dessert, as a picnic dish, as a snack, as a celebratory centrepiece, and

A cake prepared in celebration of Hitler's birthday in 1937.

Successful nuclear weapons tests at Bikini Atoll are celebrated with a cake in 1946.

as a gift. It is also probable that cake's status as indulgence, as purely unnecessary luxury, enhances its role as desirable commodity. Whatever the reason, such legendary cakes carry much of the significatory function of cake as a concept.

Nothing enhances the fame of a cake more than a long-drawn-out conflict over its recipe or origins. One of the most famously disputed cakes is the Austrian *Sachertorte*, which was the subject of a seven-year legal battle. The cake's genesis is undisputed: it was invented in the kitchens of Klemens, Prince von Metternich, in 1832. The Prince, one of the architects of the Congress of Vienna, asked his cook to invent a new dessert for a special function: a drier 'masculine' cake rather than the fluffy, 'feminine' style of *Torten* more common at the time. The chef fell ill, and one of his apprentices, the sixteen-year-old Franz Sacher, worked on the cake instead. What he came up with was a firm chocolate cake, its sweetness tempered by the tang of apricot preserves, the whole covered by a smooth, glossy chocolate glaze. While the chocolate cake recipe itself was nothing new, the glaze was an innovation, and the fame of the cake soon earned Franz Sacher a more elevated post in the kitchens of the Hungarian Prince Pál Antal Esterházy. Sacher later returned to Vienna to take up a high position in Dehne, the bakery to the emperor. It was here that he started to sell the cake to the general public. Later still he opened his own bakery, which his son expanded into a hotel which eventually became world famous. The legal dispute over the right to use the name 'the Original *Sacher Torte*' was between the Hotel Sacher and Demel's bakery (the renamed Dehne). In the lean years after the Second World War, the owners of Hotel Sacher sued Demel's in order to establish their absolute right over the 'brand' of *Sachertorte*. The court case rested on the placement of the apricot preserves. Demel's placed the preserves on top of the cake (a necessity if the chocolate glaze is to retain its glossiness when set), while Sacher's recipe also split the cake in half and sandwiched it with a further layer of preserves. After much poring over ancient recipes, the court decided in favour of Sacher, whose version of the cake now carries a chocolate medallion proclaiming its authenticity. Their cake alone can be designated as '*Sacher Torte*'. Demel countered by stating that it would market its cake as the '*Ur-Sachertorte*'. Any version of the cake is designated by the word 'Sacher' piped on top in chocolate, a symbolic seal of identity, permanently glamorizing what would otherwise seem an oddly undistinguished variety of cake.[9] Similar spats about the most authentic recipe and the original source have done much to spread the fame of Grasmere Gingerbread (more of a ginger-flavoured biscuit than the usual cake-like variety), which has been sold to visitors to the Lake District since the days of the residency of Wordsworth and Coleridge.

Then there are cakes that are famous because of their literary connections. Lady Baltimore Cake, a speciality of the Southern states of America, first achieved fame through its appearance in a novel by popular romantic novelist Owen Wister in 1906. The title of *Lady Baltimore*, set in Charleston, South Carolina, refers not to a person but to a cake, around which much of the action of the novel revolves. The narrator first tries the cake in a teashop after hearing a hapless young man order it for his forthcoming wedding:

> 'I should like a slice, if you please, of Lady Baltimore', I said with extreme formality . . . I returned to the table and she brought me the cake, and I had my first felicitous meeting with Lady Baltimore. Oh, my goodness! Did you ever taste it? It's all soft, and it's in layers, and it has nuts – but I can't write any more about it; my mouth waters too much. Delighted surprise caused me once more to speak aloud, and with my mouth full, 'But, dear me, this is delicious.'

The narrator returns repeatedly to the teashop for further slices of the cake, and in the process becomes embroiled in the lives of the young man and the girl behind the counter. Wister's description of the cake was so appealing that fans started demanding the recipe. The cake does seem to predate the novel, appearing in the letters column of the *Ladies' Home Journal* in 1889, but it was Wister's novel that made it desirable.[10] Florence and Nina Ottelengui, who ran the Lady Baltimore Tea Rooms in Charleston for over 25 years, reportedly sent a cake in thanks to the author every Christmas. A soft, white cake, which is often served as a wedding cake, the

Lady Baltimore is topped with white, meringue-like 'seven minute' frosting, into which chopped nuts and candied fruits are stirred. Another literary-inspired cake is Dolly Varden Cake, which does not actually exist in cake form within the text which inspires it. It is named after a silly coquette in Dickens's *Barnaby Rudge* (1841), who so caught the imagination of his readers that a bizarre variety of objects were named after her, including a hat, a parasol, paper dolls, a bright spotted dress fabric, a trout, the brake van of a train, and a cake. With the exception of the brake van, these objects have in common their brightly coloured, spotted or flower-strewn appearance, resembling Dolly's mode of dress. The

Dolly Varden,
lithograph, 1872.

cake appears to have been invented by an American fan of the novel, and is very much in the American rather than the British tradition of cake-making – light and layered high – with one layer spotted with dried and candied fruits to evoke Dolly's colourful mode of dress. In recent years this cake name has been attached in America to the variety of little girl's birthday cake that consists of a cake skirt with a doll's head and torso inserted into it. The name reallocation seems to have been the initial work of an enterprising manufacturer of cake tins; it is entertaining to see the process by which a cake named after a fictional character's style of dress eventually becomes a cake in the form of a dress.

The naming of cakes serves a commemorative function in many cases. Cakes are named after the place associated with their origins (Dundee Cake, Black Forest Gateau (*Schwarzwälderkirschtorte*), Banbury Cakes), important social occasions and rituals (Election Cake, New Orleans King Cake), and, particularly, after famous people (Napoleons, Pavlova, Lamingtons, Radetzky Torte, Battenberg, Savarin, Victoria Sandwich). The history and social function of some of these cakes is particularly intriguing. Election Cake, the claim to which is contested by several different towns in Connecticut, is one of the earliest recorded American cakes, predating, in its first form, the War of Independence. It is a form of yeast-raised 'great cake', brought to America in the seventeenth century by English settlers. First known as Muster Cake, it was baked by inns and householders to serve to the farmers who arrived annually for muster day, when they would receive military training then spend the night carousing. After independence, the same cake and celebration were transferred to the annual elections. It seems possible that these celebrations served also to compensate the people for the loss of the festivals of Easter and Christmas,

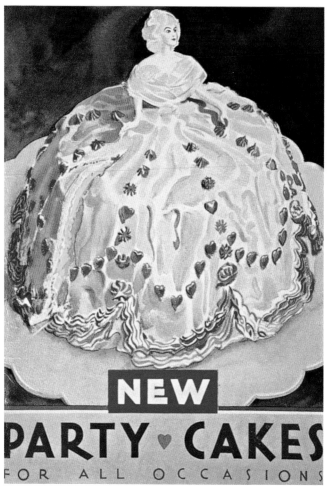

Crinoline lady cake.

which the Puritan church forbade them to celebrate, with the preparations, baking, and sharing transferred to strictly secular occasions. The importance of election day declined in the early twentieth century, with easier transport meaning that the need to feed and house travellers overnight was no longer such a key feature of the occasion. With the coming of chemical raising agents the yeast-raised form of the cake was lost, and it exists today only as an historical curiosity.

And then there is the Lamington, which is virtually the patron cake of Australia. A small square single-portion sponge cake (baked in a sheet like *petits fours* and then sliced up), a Lamington is dipped in chocolate icing and then rolled in coconut. The cakes are believed to be named after Baron Lamington, the governor of Queensland from 1896 to 1901. Different sources assign the connection either to his kitchens (claiming the cake was invented there, perhaps, prosaically, as a way to use up stale or burnt sponge cake), or to his wife

Raphaelle Peale, *Still-life with Cake*, 1818, oil on wood. Cake is a rarity in still-life compositions before the twentieth century.

Lamingtons.

(said to have a keen interest in household matters), or to a homburg hat the governor was given to wearing which allegedly resembled the cakes. Lord Lamington was said to loath his namesakes and to refer to them as 'those bloody poofy woolly biscuits'. For reasons I have been entirely unable to ascertain, Lamingtons attained the status of an institution in both Australia and New Zealand. The earliest published recipe so far known dates from 1902, when the *Queenslander* weekly newspaper published a recipe contributed by 'A Subscriber'. Fund-raising cake sales are often referred to as Lamington Drives – a nomenclature which may be evidence of the popularity of the cake or may in part contribute to it. The strong influence of British culture on Australia and New Zealand ensured that afternoon tea was for many years a significant institution, which in turn produced a highly developed culture of home baking. In recent decades, with the turn towards the Far East, such Anglocentric cultural remnants have begun to seem increasingly irrelevant to younger generations: for them, these cakes exist as objects of kitsch – relics from a past receding rapidly out of sight, rather than something they might actually eat.

3
The Culture of Baking Cake

The glory days of British home baking began in the Elizabethan period, with the management of large houses and manors passing from male stewards into the hands of the gentlewoman housewife, who became responsible for overseeing the provision of bread, beer, butter and cheese, preserving meats and vegetables, drying herbs and candying fruits. The housewife was a figure of much cultural interest in this period. Gervase Markham, author of *The English Huswife* (1615) was clear on the virtues she must possess: 'She . . . must bee cleanly in both body and garments, she must have a quick eye, a curious nose, a perfect taste and a ready ear; she must not be butter-fingered, sweet toothed nor faint hearted.'[1] This portrait is absolutely in contrast to that of the professional chef of the day, who was typically portrayed with a series of tropes surprisingly similar to those operative today – bad-tempered, foul-mouthed, authoritarian, but marvellously skilled:

> The kitchen is his hell and he the very devil in it . . . he
> will domineer and rule the roast, in spite of his master,
> and curses is the very dialect of his calling . . . His cunning
> is not small in architecture, for he builds strange fabrics in

paste, towers and castles, and like Darius his palace, in one banquet demolished.[2]

Home baking continued to be an ideal throughout the seventeenth and eighteenth centuries, and built-in ovens became more common in smaller houses. The range and complexity of baked goods increased dramatically, with sponge biscuits of all sorts, macaroons and shortcakes joining the Banbury cakes, marchpanes, jumbles, wafers, gingerbread and spice cakes of the Tudor and medieval repertoire. Yet baking, particularly of great cakes, was still a prodigious undertaking: the dried fruit had to be washed, dried and stoned, the candied peel chopped, the sugar to be cut from huge conical loaves, pounded into crumbs and then passed through a sieve. Butter was washed, eggs were beaten for a minimum of half an hour, and yeast had to be set working.

'The Confectioner', part of a series by Abraham Bosse on *Les Métiers* (the trades), engraving, *c.* 1632–5.

There was then the enormous technical challenge of baking a huge cake in a wood-fired oven without burning the outside or undercooking the centre. In England in these centuries, the country house and its cooking functioned as a cultural ideal to which others aspired. There was a great deal of continuity in its cooking: housewives kept manuscript books which they passed on to their daughters and granddaughters (food historian Florence White, writing in the 1930s, claimed that recipes of 'good epicurean country-house cookery' had been handed down in her family since the days of Elizabeth 1). The situation was by no means the same in France, where a huge social gulf separated the country and the city in the centuries before the Revolution, and where the desirable recipes were the innovatory, perfectionist dishes of the great chefs who served the court. The English housewife was crucially a gentlewoman – of high rank. Her equivalent in France is difficult to find, as the French social system operated very differently, with a much larger aristocracy than the British and a culture that looked to the court rather than to the country for its values and practices. What is clear is that the French woman of high rank in the sixteenth, seventeenth and eighteenth centuries did not occupy herself with matters of the kitchen. Cooking was a job for a man whose profession it was. The job of pâtissier was separate from that of chef in the French culinary profession, a specific trade requiring high technical skill. (A series of medieval statutes had also distinguished it from the trade of baker.) Many of the differences between English and French cakes are traceable to this fundamental distinction in their baking practices. French cakes are the product of centuries of professional refinement and perfectionism. Little masterpieces, they are showy, transitory affairs. English cakes are cakes for the household, baked once a week on a designated baking

Habit de Paticier

The pastry chef's clothes (*Habit de paticier*), a fantasy etching and engraving by Nicolas de Larmessin, part of a series of *Travestissements, c.* 1695–1720.

day, and therefore prized for their keeping qualities. They make use of simple ingredients, ideally those produced locally (on the estate in the case of those early manor houses), and part of their function is to use up materials of which there is a surplus, so pound cakes requiring many eggs would be baked when there was a glut.

As England became an increasingly urban nation in the late eighteenth and nineteenth centuries, the *ideal* of country-house baking nonetheless continued to hold sway. Baked goods of all sorts were widely available in the towns, but cakes baked at home had considerably more social cachet. The cookbooks of Eliza Acton and Isabella Beeton both have hefty chapters of cake recipes, including both sponge and pound cake varieties (Acton in fact disapproved of rich cakes, considering them 'sweet poison', but felt that her readers would not be content without a good selection of cake recipes). The theory was that these cakes would be baked by someone other than the mistress of the house. Notions of genteel leisure spread down the social scale, and by the mid-nineteenth century cookbooks are assuming that the work of the kitchen is no longer something with which the middle-class housewife is physically involved. That this is simply a polite fiction becomes obvious when one compares typical middle-class incomes with scales of wages for servants, which make it clear that a cook was only affordable for those at the very top of the scale. Most middle-class women still had to dirty their hands; what cookbooks like Mrs Beeton's offered them was the means to hide such undignified labour. Cakes were essential because the institution of afternoon tea was by now firmly established. Begun by aristocrats in the eighteenth century, it had filtered down the social scale to become a fixture of the lives of most middle-class women, for whom the weekly 'at-home day'

'Beauty in the Kitchen', an 1860 ink drawing by Jane Cook.

when they would receive friends for tea, sandwiches and cake was the centre of their social lives. The custom reached its height during the brief Edwardian age, when tea was so important a social function that women changed into special tea gowns for the occasion. Thereafter, with the lives of middle-class women becoming less leisured, and an increasing focus on health, the fashionable cake went into decline, now a snack for hikers or a tea-time treat for children (provided they had first consumed several slices of bread and butter), but no longer a social centrepiece. Baking went downmarket, becoming the province of popular women's magazines and cookery pamphlets, which continued to place great emphasis on the baking of cakes and biscuits long after more upmarket publications had ceased to do so. It is notable that during the Second World War one of the biggest complaints about food rationing was that it was no longer possible to bake cakes. Wartime food writers became increasingly ingenious in their suggestions for substitutions to make cake baking possible again, with eggs replaced by vinegar or bicarbonate of soda and sugar by carrots, beet-roots or dried milk. The point was not really to have something that tasted like cake, but that looked a bit like it – a centrepiece for the table, the reassurance that a fancy tea was still possible. So one writer gave enthusiastic directions for how to stretch a small round bought sponge or teacake

'The Little Bakers', from *A Children's Book of Trades*, c. 1870.

(preferably stale for ease of cutting) into three different cakes for six to eight people, by dint of careful cutting into smaller layers, triangles and stars and the applying of fillings and icings made variously of peanut butter and milk powder.[3] It is pretty clear that taste was not the key concern. In the post-war years cake baking lost further ground, though there was a brief revival in the 1970s on the back of the whole food movement, with wholemeal cakes, oat slices and carrot cake a feature of homespun hippyish cafes in most towns. It is probably from this moment that the modern habit of eating cake as part of lunch, to follow a sandwich and accompanied by coffee, caught on as practice among workers and shoppers in British towns and cities.

In post-revolutionary France the most significant culinary change was the development of the restaurant, with the chefs who had been employed by the great kitchens of the *ancien régime* setting up numerous establishments around Paris. The food of professional chefs rather than domestic cooking therefore reached more people and gained increasing influence on the culinary mindset of the nation. The arbiters of French culinary identity took a surprisingly long time to notice anything much beyond the environs of Paris. Food entered the capital daily from the rest of the country – 'the provinces have long paid a gastronomic tribute to the capital in the form of hams, sausages, cheeses, and fish' – but it wasn't until the end of the nineteenth century that food writers and chefs began to pay attention to provincial food.[4] With the rise of paid vacations and motoring trips in the early years of the twentieth century, Parisians began to become familiar with and to value the food of the provinces. In contrast with Britain, it was still 'commercially' produced goods that were valued, however: in the case of cakes, those produced for sale rather than those baked in the home. The idealized peasant producer is imagined as an artisan, selling the fruits of her skill, rather than as a housewife, feeding her family. Cakes were baked in the French home, but they were considerably simpler than the elaborate confections of the pastrycook: plain undecorated chestnut, chocolate and almond cakes to be served as a dessert. But in the last decade a dramatic revolution has taken place in French home baking, with the introduction of 'le cake'. Popularized by 'Sophie' (Sophie Dudemaine, a cookbook writer with a Delia-like recognition factor in France), French 'cake' is a plainish baking-powder-raised batter of the sort that the British would use for a tea-bread (the *'simple cake aux fruits confits de nos amis anglo-saxons'*), but it is usually savoury. All sorts of flavourings are used – ham, seafood, cheeses, herbs, vegetables, cooked meats[5] – and the resultant dish is usually served in small pieces as an aperitif. Although they are also sold in supermarkets, these cakes belong to the province of the home cook rather than the professional pâtissier and represent a revolution in the relationship between the French and their cakes.[6]

It is said that a copy of Gervase Markham's *English Huswife* was taken to America on the Mayflower. It is certainly true that early American cakes (as indicated in the discussion of Election Cake) derived from the British model. The *idea* of baking is nowhere more important than in the culture of North America. Cakes rank high in the culinary hierarchy, and they come to be of particular importance in the construction of ideas of home and motherhood. It is geography that makes America a nation of home bakers. The early settlers lived in spartan, isolated communities marooned in a great wilderness. The pioneers moving west in the nineteenth century were entirely reliant on their own resources, and needed the skills to produce all the family food from sparse and locally available materials. Laura Ingalls Wilder's account

Baking with mother: the cover of a 1950s American cookbook.

of her pioneer childhood in the *Little House on the . . .* series details the hardships and pleasures of life on the frontier, in which food is the chief occupation – and preoccupation – of the family, a matter of life or death rather than pleasure. And yet, there are cakes: the 'sugar-white' frosted cake of the unpleasant Nellie Oleson's party; Laura's own wedding cake, for which she whisks the egg whites on a plate until her arm is stiffer than the whites; and the heart-shaped cakes made from white sugar and flour that the girls find one year in their Christmas stockings, objects of luxury from a distant world of urban sophistication. Cakes are rarities in pioneer life, yet they shine across the years in Ingalls's thinly fictionalized memoirs, important as representatives of something beyond subsistence, a food that is nothing but an indulgent pleasure, and yet speaks of love and community.[7] Pioneer culture still influences American attitudes to baking, with the idea of independence, of doing it yourself, one of the key values attached to the American cake. Recipes are particularized, belonging to an individual who has tweaked and personalized them – 'Mabel's Sugar-Frosted Chocolate Loaf Cake', 'Sue-Ellen's Pineapple-Peppermint-Peach Delight'. Secret recipes and tricks abound, with stories of relatives who take their unique recipe for Devil's Food Cake to the grave. The names of the cakes that won prizes in the famous Pillsbury Grand National Bake-Off hark back repeatedly to images of the frontier and the great trek west: 'This recipe came to me from a darling Southern gentlewoman who was one of the early pioneers in Arizona', says Mrs Richard W. Sprague of California of her $4,000 winning 'Aunt Carrie's BonBon Cake', a third-prize winner in the first year of the competition; while Mrs Vava M. Blackburn of Walla Walla won $1,000 for her 'Gold Rush Cake' three years later. Launched in 1949, the Bake-Off was a nationwide competition in celebration of the culinary skills of American women, with a particular focus on baking: pies, cookies, tray-bakes and cakes jostled for the big prizes, which went up to $50,000 dollars in the early years – a truly astounding amount of money for the 'No-Knead Water-Rising Nut Twists' which won in 1949. The titles of American recipes tell us a great deal about the unique baking culture of the nation; there is an over-riding concern with two issues: method and origins. If the method is labour-saving, or particularly quick, or in any way unusual, this will be heralded in the recipe's title: 'Hurry-Up Cake', 'Half-Hour Chocolate Cake', 'Mystery Cake' (all from Irma Rombauer's classic *The Joy of Cooking*). A great favourite to this day is 'Dump Cake', in which the ingredients (all from cans and packets) are simply dumped in a tin and baked, unstirred, with a cake mysteriously forming itself in the oven. If a recipe can be traced back to an ancestor, or to an important period of American history, or to a country of ethnic origin, that too will be heralded in the title.

The prime virtues in American cakes are height and lightness of texture. The layer cake is considered a national invention ('After a long period abroad nothing could make me more homesick or emotional than an American maga-zine advertisement of a luscious layer cake'[8]), although it clearly has much in common with the *gâteaux* and *Torten* of France, Germany and Austria, and even with the Victoria Sandwich of Britain. The crucial point of the layer cake is that its fillings and frostings are as important as the cake, rather than an optional addition, as in the cakes of the British tradition. Multiple layers will be piled high, with the filling (usually a variant of buttercream) often as deep as the layers of cake it is piled between, and a thick frosting covers the sides and top of the cake, where it will be swirled up as much as an inch. Angel Cake, which dates from the nineteenth

Cake, Lemon, Strawberries and Glass, oil on canvas, 1890, by John Peto, an American artist known for his *trompe-l'oeil* paintings.

century, is a uniquely American institution – a sponge cake raised with the whites of eggs and baking powder, containing no yolks or butter, so that it is nothing but light, white, airy texture.

Valuing ease and ingenuity of method, according high status to the home-baked cake, and preoccupied above all with verticality and airiness, the American home baker was ripe for the assault on her practices mounted by manufacturers in the early twentieth century. The first manufactured cake mixes went on sale in the early 1930s. They contained everything required to make a cake: the housewife just had to add water and stir. That these were not instantly successful has much to do with the unique place accorded to cake in the American cultural imagination. It is a sentimental object, imagined first and foremost as embodying an act of love, an offering of time and skill, sweetness and pleasure by the mother to her family. Too much ease and convenience might dilute the worth of this love. The psychologist Dr Ernest Dichter, consulted by General Mills flour company, felt that the problem could be solved if the dried eggs were removed and the housewife was herself required to add an egg. The solution was successful (perhaps because it hit the right emotional buttons, or maybe because the taste of the dried eggs had been too unpleasant), and cake mixes gained gradual, inexorable cultural ascendancy from the 1950s onwards, with even Mamie Eisenhower instructing her cooking staff to make use of this novel invention at the White House. Manufacturers, who advertised extensively, and even co-opted serious food writers such as James Beard to their campaigns, devised the phrase 'from scratch' to refer to a cake prepared the conventional way, and succeeded in convincing the American woman that the baking of the cake was just the first, tedious part of the operation. With that

Cake contest at an American Electric Center, 1938.

taken off her hands she could concentrate on the really creative operation of filling and frosting and decorating: 'Now, success in cakemaking is packaged right along with the precision ingredients. You can put your effort into glorifying your cake with frosting, dreaming up an exciting trim that puts your own label on it.'[9] A glance at any of the numerous home-baking blogs in which self-styled 'soccer moms' post records of their creations makes clear the extent to which cake mixes are still today an established way of life, and 'scratch cakes' as eccentric as the disease-evoking name implies. One of the great successes in American baking books of the last few years has been the *Cake Doctor* series, which suggests ways to create original, exciting cakes by gussying up cake mixes with added ingredients. To simply do away with the cake mix altogether does not seem to be a viable option, but it is still of vital importance that the cake should be 'home-baked'.[10]

4
The Rituals and
Symbolism of Cake

The cake of our collective imagination is round. But why? Why does the flat-topped cylinder speak 'cake' across times and cultures? There are practical reasons to do with evenness of baking (the corners of a straight-sided cake will become dry sooner and burn more quickly), but the roundness of cakes may also have a symbolic significance. Comparative anthropology and mythography have found evidence of round cakes in virtually all cultures and periods. And they very often serve a specific ritual function. For over a thousand years the Chinese have eaten moon cakes to celebrate the mid-Autumn festival. The ritual involves families gathering together to eat quarters of the small cakes, drink wine, recite poetry and watch the moon. Traditionally these pastries are round, a shape designed to echo that of the full moon. Denser than Western baked goods, they consist of a firm filling surrounded by a thin pastry shell. The filling can now range from sausage to birds' nests to dried flowers, but originally consisted of lotus seed paste or a sweetened bean curd, sometimes with preserved salted egg yolks embedded in the centre. The egg yolks symbolize the full moon, as does the pastry itself, and the symbols with which it is decorated. Moon cakes have a legendary as well as a mythic significance, with many stories circulating about their use in rebellions against the Mongol rulers in the fourteenth century: one version has weapons hidden inside huge cakes; another, more convincingly, claims that messages were hidden inside the cakes which could then be passed to others without arousing the suspicions of the hated authorities.

Round cakes are particularly linked to annual festivals marking the cycle of the year. While the ancient Chinese celebrated the huge round harvest moon in Autumn, the pagan Russians baked flat round 'sun cakes' in honour of the return of the sun in springtime. The festival of Maslenitsa marked the vernal equinox until the Orthodox church moved it to coincide with Lent. Lasting fourteen days, the festival centred on the baking of hot round yellow pancakes. With elaborate rituals on each day involving the sharing of pancakes with relatives (sons-in-law with their mothers-in-law, wives with their sisters-in-law), the celebrations used the symbolic foods to bind extended families as well as to celebrate the return of spring. The ancient Celts seem also to have marked the seasons with round cakes. The festival of

Modern Chinese moon cakes.

Beltane on 1 May, which celebrates the coming of summer, could involve several cake-based rituals: in one a round cake was formed with knobs all over its top. The cake was baked on the edge of the Beltane fire and then broken into sections of a knob each and shared among the company. The person who received the specially charred portion became the symbolic sacrifice who had to jump three times through the fire. Another ritual involved the baking of a large cake which was rolled downhill, its passage echoing the passing of the sun across the sky. The cake was broken and shared out at the bottom of the hill.[1]

More recent cakes also have their ritual functions, some of which involve the roundness of the cake, and some its function as an object to be cut or broken and shared. One of the most complexly symbolic of cakes is Twelfth Cake, or Twelfth Night Cake, also known as King Cake or *Galette des Rois*. The feast of Epiphany on 6 January was observed in similar ways throughout medieval Europe. A cake would be baked in which a bean was placed (said to represent the infant Christ). The person whose share of the cake contained the bean would be king for a night. In elaborate versions of the festivities he could appoint courtiers, such as a jester. Sometimes a pea was also included, to identify the queen. Whenever the king took a drink the entire company would follow suit, shouting 'the king drinks!' This early tradition was elaborated in different ways in different cultures; many of these cakes still exist. The *Dreikönigskuchen* of Germany and Switzerland is a wreath of rich bread in which an almond is concealed. Spain's ring-shaped *roscón de reyes* is decorated with candied fruits and contains a *sorpresa* – a coin or small ceramic figure which is said to bring luck to the finder. There are similar cakes in Portugal and Mexico: in the former case the next year's *bolo rei* is to be provided by the finder of the bean; in the latter the finder of the china doll must give a party at Candlemas. The Mexican custom resembles that of New Orleans, whose famous King Cake (brioche-like and smothered in gold, green and purple icing) contains a plastic baby whose finder must host the next party. One of the most elaborate versions of the tradition is that practised in France around the *Galette des rois*, a rich confection whose golden, scalloped puff pastry encloses a dense almond filling. In the typical French ritual, one of the children of the family hides under the table and calls out the names of those assembled in a random order to determine who receives which slice of cake. This deliberate confusing of hierarchy recalls the origins of the tradition in the Roman feast of Saturnalia, where servants played at being masters and masters servants and the finding of a bean or token, or the throw of a dice, bestowed temporary kingship.

Jacob Jordaens, *The Bean King*, *c.* 1655, oil on canvas.

The feast of Epiphany became a popular genre subject for painters in the seventeenth century. The first to tackle the theme appears to have been the Antwerp painter Jacob Jordaens, whose depiction of *The Bean King* (*c.* 1655) shows a rowdy gathering in the midst of toasting the old man who has been crowned king. Over a hundred years later, in Jean-Baptiste Greuze's *Epiphany (Le gâteau des rois)* of 1774, the scene is one of idealized domestic calm, as the children of a peasant family search pieces of cake for the glory-conferring bean. The shift in the focus of the scene from adults to children, drunkenness to calmness, may map a growing cultural anxiety about the celebration in Protestant Europe. It was concern at the pagan origins of the feast that eventually put paid to the British Twelfth Cake. This version was a fruit cake – yeast-raised in earlier periods. After the Reformation the church removed Twelfth Night as a religious festival; it was revived as a purely secular feast in the late

Jean-Baptiste Greuze, *Le gâteau des rois*, 1774, oil on canvas.

seventeenth century, when a series of tokens began to be included in the cake. Henry Teonge, a naval captain, described in 1676 a Twelfth Cake and associated celebration enjoyed at sea:

> We had much mirth on board, for we had a great cake made, in which was put a bean for the king, a pea for the queen, a clove for a knave, a forked stick for the cuckold and a rag for the slut. The cake was cut into several pieces in the great cabin, and all put into a napkin, out of which everyone took his piece, as out of a lottery; then each piece is broken to see what was in it, which caused much laughter, to see our Lieutenant prove the cuckold, and more to see us tumble one over the other in the cabin, by reason of the rough weather.[2]

The tokens in the eighteenth century became a series of figures printed on paper which were cut out and drawn from a hat. In the nineteenth century manufacturers started to construct the figures from card and plaster, and confectioners from almond paste and icing, elaborately moulded and coloured, and they were displayed on top of the cake, often in elaborate scenes. The Twelfth Cake with its galaxy of figures was so ubiquitous in Victorian culture that it appeared frequently in the work of contemporary political cartoonists. So a cartoon in *The Penny Satirist* of Saturday, 9 January 1841 entitled 'Twelfth Night; or The Imps of the Cake' has the cake as the nation, being devoured by its own decorations, with a useful guide to the characters appended beneath: 'Foreigners Feed on it, Germans Gnaw it, Hanover Halves it . . . Kings Keep it, Lawyers Lick it.' Nearly half a century later the trope is still going strong, with a cartoon in *Fun* on 9 January 1884 entitled 'The Grand Twelfth Cake for the

Isaac Cruikshank, *Drawing for Twelfth-Cake at St Annes Hill*, 1799, hand-coloured etching.

Million, W. E. Gladstone, Confectioner', with a baker staggering under the weight of an enormous Twelfth Cake with figures representing Britannia sitting on a weary Gladstonian lion, and banners proclaiming municipal and electoral reform. By this date, the Twelfth Cake itself was no more: the new rites and rituals of Christmas, introduced into Britain by Victoria and Albert in the 1840s, had by the 1870s completely displaced the older festival. The Twelfth Cake was replaced by (some would say, mutated into) the Christmas cake – still a rich fruit cake with almond and royal icing, but no longer bearing those symbolic figures.

The British Christmas cake, like many of our most treasured rituals of the season, is not, therefore, very old at all. It has, though, acquired a notable presence as a symbolically necessary component of the festivities. In the nineteenth and early twentieth centuries long-lasting fruit cake was frequently sent by the British to relatives in the 'colonies' overseas, often as part of the contents of a Christmas hamper. In North

America in the early twentieth century enterprising grocers produced a variety of fruitcake covered in a dense mosaic of glistening preserved fruits and nuts, which became a popular seasonal gift for distant friends and relatives. Today the 'British-style' fruitcake has become notorious, with comedians offering riffs on the everlasting cake (Johnny Carson suggested that there was only one fruitcake in existence, forever gifted to new ungrateful recipients). If the symbolic import of Twelfth Cake is in the act of division and sharing, the symbolic significance of its descendant is in its indivisibility, with endless accounts of impenetrably rock-like royal icing (professional bakers add a spoonful of glycerine to avert this calamity). In the American context the problem with fruit cake is that it is the opposite of what now registers as 'cake' in the popular imagination. If 'cake' is soft, tall, light, fluffy and ephemeral then a cake that is solid, dense and seemingly everlasting poses a conceptual problem. Another interesting take on the symbolism of Christmas cake is that offered by modern Japan, where the celebratory cake is a light perishable substance, often containing strawberries or chocolate. Until recently women who remained unmarried after the age of 25 were referred to as 'Christmas cakes', as they had passed their likely use-by date. (In a recognition of changing times the age limit has since been shifted to 31, with the insult transferred to *toshikoshi-soba*, a noodle dish traditionally eaten on 31 December.)

The contemporary cake that is most heavily ritualized is the wedding cake. Mary Douglas remarked that 'a competent young anthropologist, arriving on this planet from Mars' would be more struck by the rituals surrounding the cutting and distributing of wedding cake than he would by the Japanese tea ceremony, and would 'be perhaps baffled to make up his mind whether the central focus of the ceremony was the marriage or the cake'.[3] There is a great deal of food-lore about the history of the wedding cake, which is often traced back to ancient Roman traditions of breaking bread over the head of the bride or to the medieval British tradition of pouring grain over the heads of the newly married couple. But the wedding cake as we understand it did not even start to come into existence until the late eighteenth century, and much of its accretion of ritual and symbol is of surprisingly recent origin.[4] Although cakes were certainly served as part of wedding feasts from the Middle Ages onward, they were not specifically designated as 'bride cakes'. The first recipe to be so named seems to have been that given by Elizabeth Raffald in her *The Experienced English Housekeeper* of 1769, which is for a fairly rich, not overly sweet fruit cake, banded by layers of candied peel. Bride cakes are mentioned in cookery books throughout the later eighteenth and particularly the nine-teenth century, but there is not – as now – any distinctive recipe that denotes a wedding cake: they are simply large, somewhat rich fruit cakes. The 'traditional' British wedding cake as we understand it today is covered first in an almond paste and then with hard white royal icing; there are usually also piped icing decorations, white on white. It is in tiers, con-ventionally three, usually separated by pillars. The cake will be ritually displayed, usually on its own table, then cut by the bride and groom together; it will then be divided into small portions, some to be consumed at the wedding by the guests and others to be packaged into small boxes for absent friends and relations. The top tier of the cake may be put aside to be saved for the christening of the first child.

Wedding cakes remained single-tiered until the middle of the nineteenth century. Queen Victoria's in 1840 was 'a great beast of a plum-cake' three yards (2.7 m) in circumfer-ence and weighing 300 pounds (136 kg), but it was a single

Queen Elizabeth's wedding cake, 1947.

A two-tier bride's cake.

flat cake. It was the wedding cake of her daughter, the Princess Royal, in 1858 that changed things. It excited intense popular interest, with a picture published in the *Illustrated London News* and reports throughout the national press. This much-admired and much-imitated cake was only cake in part. Of the three tiers that made up its nearly seven-foot (2.1 m) height, only the bottom one was cake. The top layers were elaborate architectural structures – domes and crowns, plinths and niches, statues and plaques – formed entirely of sugar work. Such sugar craft demanded enormous technical skill and was consequently extremely expensive, and within the financial reach only of the most wealthy. Ordinary people, also wanting the grandeur of tall cakes, made do with cakes piled on top of each other to produce an approximation of the towering structures graced by royalty. The pillars came later still, to give the cake more height and elegance.

As the term 'bride cake' suggests, the cake is in some sense understood to stand in for the bride herself. Some modern accounts of the wedding cake assume that the bride and groom joining hands to plunge the knife into the cake is an ancient symbol for the breaking of the bride's hymen. In fact this practice is one of the most recent innovations in the symbolic catalogue of the wedding cake. Abundant sources throughout the nineteenth century assume that the job of

The bride cuts the wedding cake alone in this early nineteenth-century image of a small wedding.

cutting the cake for the guests to share is that of the wife alone. It is only in the 1930s that we start to find evidence that the new husband is to join his wife, with the symbolism suggesting that this shared task stands in for the joint work of the marriage to come. The practical reason for this innovation is that icing hard enough to support the upper layers of cake and pillars is too hard to slice with any ease.

The wedding cake has two fundamental functions, their distinction indicated by their temporal separation in the wedding reception: its first role is an object to be seen, its elegance and elevation lending it a fairytale appearance; something dream-like, impossible. As such, it speaks of the liminality of the wedding day itself – a transitory state between two more prosaic realities. Its second function is much more ancient: it is a substance to be cut and shared, so that the good fortune of the couple be shared with the guests, and the good wishes of the guests with the couple. It is a version of breaking bread together, one of the oldest of all human food rituals. It is complicated in the modern wedding by its overlap with another set of practices to do with the use of wedding cake as a divination device, which girls could put under their pillows in order to dream of a future husband. In the late eighteenth century a variation on this procedure arises, with small pieces of the cake being passed through the wedding ring before being distributed to the bride's unmarried friends. It is this that is represented in John Everett Millais's highly eroticized 1851 painting of 'The Bridesmaid', in which the girl in question, glowing red hair unbound and dominating the picture with its luxuriant waves, passes a portion of cake through a ring with an expression of barely restrained passionate yearning. The idea of keeping the top tier for the christening of the first child belongs to the twentieth century, a practical notion inspired by the fact that fruit cake 'matures' rather than rots with age.

John Everett Millais, *The Bridesmaid*, 1851, oil on panel.

The British wedding cake tradition strongly influenced practices in North America, where a similar range of rituals are observed. The main difference is that the American tradition has two cakes – a white bride's cake and a dark groom's cake. The dark/light structure of the British cake –

A cake to celebrate an anniversary of the American women's suffrage movement, 1916.

dark, rich cake and white icing – is split between the two American cakes: the groom's cake is dark – once a fruit cake, but more often today a chocolate cake – while the bride's cake is light, pale and fluffy. The bride's cake is cut and shared at the wedding while the groom's cake is saved to be distributed later. In Australia, also heavily influenced by British ritual and baking practices, the wedding cake evolved a particular form in recent years, characterized by the use of 'plastic' paste icing and elaborate edible flowers. Both American and Australian cakes have fed back into British practices through the influence of magazines, cookbooks and celebrity weddings, and such light, brightly-coloured and ornate cakes are now very often found as the centrepieces of British weddings. Regardless of its differences in form, one thing remains true of the wedding cake – that it is one of the key examples of a cake whose function is to be seen rather

A mid-twentieth-century image of a children's birthday party.

than to be eaten. This is most clearly demonstrated by one of the most striking forms the cake has taken: in modern Japan the fashion for Western-style weddings is accommodated by the invention of an entirely inedible cake – with elaborate icing of wax or moulded rubber. The entire point of the cake is the slot in the back of it, into which the bride and groom plunge the ceremonial knife while their picture is taken. Sometimes a device inside the cake issues forth a cloud of steam at the dramatic moment. If such a cake seems bizarre, we need only turn to the Britain of the Second World War, where 'iced' cardboard wedding cakes were supplied by bakers for exactly the same purpose: to make a good show in the wedding pictures.[5] Having your cake rather than eating it is sometimes the most important thing.[6]

5
Literary Cakes

[O]ne day in winter . . . my mother, seeing that I was cold,
offered me some tea, a thing I did not ordinarily take . . . She
sent for one of those squat, plump little cakes called 'petites
madeleines,' which look as though they had been moulded in the
fluted valve of a scallop shell . . . I raised to my lips a spoonful of
the tea in which I had soaked a morsel of the cake. No sooner
had the warm liquid mixed with the crumbs touched my palate
than a shudder ran through me and I stopped, intent upon the
extraordinary thing that was happening to me. An exquisite
pleasure had invaded my senses, something isolated, detached,
with no suggestion of its origin . . . And suddenly the memory
revealed itself. The taste was that of the little piece of madeleine
which on Sunday mornings at Combray . . . when I went to say
good morning to her in her bedroom, my aunt Léonie used to
give me, dipping it first in her own cup of tea or tisane.

—Marcel Proust, *A La Recherche du temps perdu* (1913–27)[1]

When we think of cakes in literature two examples spring
inevitably to mind: Proust's madeleine, and the wedding cake
of Miss Havisham in Dickens's *Great Expectations*. The tropes
employed to represent these iconic cakes tell us virtually
everything we need to know about the attitudes to cake in

particular – and perhaps food in general – in the national literary traditions to which they belong. For Proust's alter ego, Swann, the madeleine is important as a conjurer of lost childhood memories, a direct sensory conduit to the past. He evokes the form of the little cake with scrupulous detail – 'the little scallop-shell of pastry, so richly sensual under its

A pile of madeleines.

severe, religious folds' – but its characteristic appearance is not significant in terms of its evocative power. Swann has seen such cakes many times in the windows of patisseries, but it is only when he tastes the cake crumbs dissolved in lime-tea that he is overwhelmed by a flood of past memory and sensation. There is nothing intrinsically portentous about this cake – it is diminutive, light and relatively dry (it can be soaked in liquid without entirely dissolving). It is a snack rather than a centrepiece; a frippet; an unnecessary and unremarkable brief indulgence. It is, in fact, barely there: a light, spongy morsel dipped in a translucent, delicately perfumed infusion. Swann does nothing so vulgar as actually *eat* the cake – he sips at a few crumbs suspended in tea. The transformative memory overwhelms him at first taste, rather than when he chews or swallows. This has nothing to do with hunger, with being full. The fugitive barely-there nature of the madeleine is absolutely the point. It is notable that Swann does not normally take tea, and does so on this occasion almost against his own will: 'I declined at first, and then, for no particular reason, changed my mind.' The keynote of the whole experience is its ephemerality.

In striking contrast, Miss Havisham's monstrous wedding cake refuses to yield to the processes of time. Uncut and uneaten, it remains, a grotesque symbol of her decaying, unwanted virginity, in central pride of place on the table set for her wedding many years before:

> The most prominent object was a long table with a tablecloth spread on it, as if a feast had been in preparation when the house and clocks all stopped together. An epergne or centrepiece of some kind was in the middle of this cloth; it was so heavily overhung with cobwebs that its form was quite undistinguishable; and, as I

Miss Havisham shows Pip her wedding cake, in the 1946 film of *Great Expectations*.

looked along the yellow expanse out of which I remember its seeming to grow, like a black fungus, I saw speck-
led-legged spiders with blotchy bodies running home to
it, and running out from it, as if some circumstance of
the greatest public importance had just transpired in the
spider community . . .

'What do you think that is?' she asked me, again
pointing with her stick; 'that, where those cobwebs are?'

'I can't guess what it is, ma'am.'

'It's a great cake. A bride-cake. Mine!'[2]

Black with mould rather than white with icing, the cake
works as a compound symbol, collapsing together notions
of unfulfilled femininity, the stranglehold of social snobbery, and the emptiness of tradition. The centrepiece of a
rite of passage that never happened, the cake lurks menac-
ingly, the home of dark scuttling creatures, eaten away from

the inside as Miss Havisham is by her poisonous campaign of revenge against the male sex. Miss Havisham's phrasing – 'A bride-cake. Mine!' – points to the sense in which the cake stands in for the body of the bride herself. The plunging of the knife into the cake by the bride seems to have become a part of the ceremony at wedding breakfasts before the date at which Dickens was writing; a practice which if it doesn't evoke the taking of the bride's virginity does suggest the surrendering of her old identity. Miss Havisham's cake is not, of course, cut. Instead of the cake taking her place, she takes the cake's: fatally injured in a fire, she is laid to die on the table that had held her wedding feast, her ravaged body in the place of the ruined cake.

The two extremes of cake-dom are here represented: the cake as monumental, symbolic centrepiece, and the cake as unnecessary indulgent snack; the public cake, whose slicing and sharing solemnizes ritual, and the individually moulded, virtually bite-sized cake whose consumption is an essentially private affair. In both cases, the cakes have emblematic significance for the novel as a whole: the massive work of memory that is central to Proust's huge novel sequence is initiated by the delicate, transitory experience of tasting the madeleine, while the female lives sacrificed on the altar of tradition and snobbery in *Great Expectations* are absolutely encapsulated in the Gothic monstrosity of the rotting wedding cake. Furthermore, the culinary identities of England and France are also exemplified by these cakes. In mid-Victorian England the wedding cake is a fairly new symbol of bourgeois respectability, a recently constructed tradition of the commercial age. The madeleine, in contrast, is a regional speciality, a product of the town of Commercy in northeastern France, and a reminder of the extent to which French food retained its regional specificity and pre-industrial

Children looking longingly through the window of a patisserie, 1950.

roots well into the twentieth century. But the most crucial distinction is the fact that Proust's madeleine is consumed, and Dickens's bride cake is not (or at least, not by the humans for whom it was intended). It is in this way that these texts most fully encapsulate national identity: the cakes of French literature are very much for eating, represented through tropes of pleasure, plenty and nostalgia, while the English tradition is full of cakes that cannot or should not be eaten, with an anxiety about pleasure and indulgence that leaves the reader with his or her nose pressed eternally to the pastry-cook's window.

Proust's madeleine is so powerfully significatory that it tends to overwhelm all other aspects of his text. But he writes of other cakes. There is the majestic chocolate cake served to the narrator by his love Gilberte at frivolous private tea-parties: 'an architectural cake, as gracious and sociable as it was imposing', a 'Babylonish pastry' from the crumbling monument of which Gilberte 'extracted for [him] a whole glazed slab jeweled with scarlet fruits, in the oriental style.'[3] Unlike the fugitive madeleine, Gilberte's monumental cake is drama incarnate, its 'oriental' form suggesting the exotic and the sexual. This is cake as pleasure, both in its elaborate form and its destruction. It offers the possibilities of play for adults – both the playing at battles suggested by the elaborate military metaphors, and the sensual play of feeding each other. Above all, this is cake to be eaten: its architectural splendours no match for Gilberte, who triumphantly reduces it to its proper form as food. Cake, later in the novel sequence, becomes *the* food for Swann, a means back to his past. When picnicking with friends, he refuses the sandwiches and will eat only cakes – 'a single chocolate cake, sugared with gothic tracery, or an apricot tart': 'This was because, with the sandwiches of cheeses and salad, a form of food that was novel to me and knew nothing of the past, I had nothing in common. But the cakes understood, the tarts were gossips. There were in the former an insipid taste of cream, in the latter a fresh taste of fruit which knew all about Combray, and about Gilberte.'[4] Proust's sense of cakes as alive is echoed in Jean-Paul Sartre's description of the cakes of different nations as people, quoted in chapter Two: a sensibility which takes pleasure in the cake as entity, as unique form. Cakes are primarily objects of pleasure in French writing – both to contemplate and to eat. The Marquis de Sade, writing to his wife in 1778 from his prison cell in the Bastille, is deeply preoccupied with the details of the chocolate cakes he wishes her to order for him: they 'ought to have the same taste as when you bite into a bar of chocolate', while Colette, in whose writings perverse culinary tastes (for rotten bananas, lime buds, the gum on fruit trees, pencil leads, chalk and rubber) suggest a louche sexuality, places cakes as part of this lexicon of the capriciously, pleasurably wanton, with her protagonist Claudine, still incorrigible in middle age, insisting on her right to devour cream cakes topped with praline regardless of the effect on her figure.[5] And then there is the elaborate cake produced for Madame Bovary's much-regretted wedding:

> They had brought in a pastry-cook from Yvetot for the tarts and the cakes. Because he was new to the district, he had taken great pains; and at dessert he appeared in person, carrying an elaborate confection that drew loud cries. At the base, to begin with, there was a square of blue cardboard, representing a temple with porticoes, colonnades and stucco statuettes all around, in little niches decorated with gold paper stars; then on the second layer there was a castle made of Savoy cake, encircled by tiny fortifications of angelica, almonds, raisins and segments of orange; and finally, on the upper platform, a green field with rocks and pools of jam and boats made out of nutshells, there was arrayed a little Cupid, perched on a chocolate swing, its two poles finished off with two real rose-buds, just like knobs, on the top.[6]

A provincial version of the grand *pièces montées* of Carême, this wedding cake serves many functions within the novel, its tripartite form echoing the tripling structures of the text

A simple *pièce montée.*

itself: three parts of the novel, three significant banquets, three men in Emma's life, three coffins. Despite its architectural and sculptural intricacies it, like Gilberte's chocolate cake, is a cake for eating. It comes at the culmination of a feast notable for its rustic generosity – groaning tables are laid out in the wagon shed bearing sirloins, legs of mutton, a sucking pig, chitterlings, jugs of brandy and cider, and huge dishes of shuddering yellow custard. The guests eat all day, leaving the table at intervals and then returning to eat more. The cake, in its excess, its plenitude, is a part of this traditional process of feasting, and yet there is a pathos in its aping of the fashionable excesses of the city and the court, in the failure of its flimsy cardboard, tinsel and jam to approach the magnificence of the structures produced by the masters of patisserie. In its clumsy aspiration, its dreaming of more, it is a harbinger of Emma's own fatal dissatisfactions.

The contrast between the cakes of French and English literature is made abundantly clear if we turn now to another wedding cake. Jane Austen's *Emma* (1815) begins with the wedding of the eponymous heroine's governess, Miss Taylor. Emma Woodhouse's father, for whom the adjective valetudinarian might have been invented, fusses about the wedding as a whole, and about the wedding cake in particular:

> There was no recovering Miss Taylor – nor much likelihood of ceasing to pity her: but a few weeks brought some alleviation to Mr Woodhouse. The compliments of his neighbours were over; he was no longer teased by being wished joy of so sorrowful an event; and the wedding-cake, which had been a great distress to him, was all ate up. His own stomach could bear nothing rich, and he could never believe other people to be different from himself. What was unwholesome to him he regarded as unfit for any body; and he had, therefore, earnestly tried to dissuade them from having any wedding-cake at all, and when that proved vain, as earnestly tried to prevent any body's eating it.[7]

So concerned is Mr Woodhouse about the possible ill effects of the cake on the stomachs of the guests that he consults the apothecary, Mr Perry, who 'could not but acknowledge (though it seemed rather against the bias of inclination) that wedding-cake might certainly disagree with many – perhaps with most people, unless taken moderately'. We never see the wedding cake – it exists not, like Emma Bovary's *pièce montée*, as a site of spectacle and fantasy, but as a source of social unease and potential indigestion. But with her customary irony, Austen rescues some iota of pleasure from this contentious cake, ending the chapter with a sly sentence:

'There was a strange rumour in Highbury of all the little Perrys being seen with a slice of Mrs Weston's wedding-cake in their hands: but Mr Woodhouse would never believe it.'

Other nineteenth-century British writers also present cake as something not to be eaten. The ladies of Elizabeth Gaskell's *Cranford* (1853), who live in reduced circumstances, see cake as an unnecessary indulgence, out of step with their code of elegant economy. When Miss Betty Barker, the jumped-up ex-seamstress, hosts a lavish tea party to curry favour with the ladies of the town, the narrator expects covert disapproval of the spread she provides:

> The tea-tray was abundantly loaded. I was pleased to see it, I was so hungry; but I was afraid the ladies might think it vulgarly heaped up. I know they would have done at their own houses; but somehow the heaps disappeared here. I saw Mrs Jamieson eating seed-cake, slowly and considerately, as she did everything; and I was rather surprised, for I knew she had told us, on the occasion of her last party, that she never had it in her house, it reminded her so much of scented soap. She always gave us Savoy biscuits. However Mrs Jamieson was kindly indulgent to Miss Barker's want of knowledge of the customs of high life; and to spare her feelings, ate three large pieces of seed-cake, with a placid, ruminating expression, not unlike a cow's.[8]

Because cake is a financial indulgence, the Cranford ladies, with their peculiar face-saving codes, have tacitly declared it to be socially undesirable. Miss Betty Barker's largesse, then, far from offering her a full *entrée* into Cranford society, serves only to mark her status as social outsider. The ladies eat the cake, telling themselves that they are too well-mannered to make this exclusion overt, but narrator Mary Smith, the outsider from the big city whose liminal position serves throughout the book to both mock and mourn the disappearing way of life of the Cranford ladies, makes it clear that the cake is really a much-appreciated addition to their meagre diet. The comedy of the contrast between Mrs Jamieson's stewardship of the 'knowledge and customs of high life' and the bovine nature of her expression as she chews the cake makes this double attitude ironically clear.

Despite its existence as a locus of social climbing and hypocrisy, Miss Betty Barker's cake does afford pleasure, though in a rather equivocal form, given that it is said to taste of soap. This passage is typical of the treatment of cake in the English literary tradition. The only notable exceptions (as is perhaps suggested by the pleasure the children take in Mrs Weston's wedding cake) are to be found in the pages of books concerning themselves with children and childhood. There are a number of cakes in Lewis Carroll's Alice books. A cake is the first thing Alice eats in Wonderland – 'a very small cake on which the words "EAT ME" were beautifully marked in currants.' Like many of the foods she encounters or hears tell of on her adventures (roast meat, turtle soup, lobsters, oysters), the cake belongs to a category of food that was forbidden (or, at least, severely restricted) for the Victorian child: food that therefore came very close to the realm of the fantastic. Much of the fantasy in this, as in many later children's books, is of exotic, unlimited food (a number of commentators have suggested that food fills the role in children's literature that sex does in adult). One of the many paradoxes of the books, however, is that this tempting plenitude is rarely available for consumption: most of the food gets whisked away from under Alice's nose – often because it possesses agency and so cannot belong to the category of the consumable ('it is rude to cut someone to whom one has been introduced', Alice is told of the joint of beef). One striking exception is the little cake – which, though it seems to possess a putative identity ('eat *me*') is positively desirous of being consumed. Alice assumes that the cake will have the opposite effect of the bottle marked "DRINK ME", which had caused her to shrink, but at first nothing happens:

> She ate a little bit, and said anxiously to herself, 'Which way? Which way?' holding her hand on the top of her head to feel which way it was growing, and she was quite surprised to find that she remained the same size: to be sure, this generally happens when one eats cake, but Alice had got so much into the way of expecting nothing

John Tenniel's illustration of the Lion and the Unicorn with a plum cake in Lewis Carroll's *Through the Looking Glass* of 1872. For contemporaries the caricatures were obvious: the aged Lion resembles Gladstone and the dandyish Unicorn Disraeli – which makes the plum cake over which they fight the nation.

A bad boy with a cake on Pleasure Island in Walt Disney's *Pinocchio* (1940).

but out-of-the-way things to happen, that it seemed quite dull and stupid for life to go on in the common way.[9]

The cake does shortly affect her size, causing her to open up like a telescope. It is clear to Alice that cake is a magical substance – on her next encounter with it (as she lies, trapped and enormous in the White Rabbit's house, being pelted through the window with pebbles that turn into cakes) she is immediately certain of its transformative power: "'If I eat one of these cakes,' she thought, 'it's sure to make *some* change in my size'." It is interesting that the only other comestibles that cause Alice to grow or shrink are drink and the (magic) mushroom. This seems to place cake in a category of inebriating, mind- as well as body- altering substances: pleasurable, but to be approached with caution.

The association of cakes with childhood is also made explicit in the work of Katherine Mansfield. Repeatedly in her short stories cakes are represented nostalgically, a childhood indulgence doomed to be left behind by the young girls she depicts hovering at the border of adulthood. So in 'The Young Girl' (1922), the unnamed seventeen-year-old of the title, awkward in her desperation for adult sophistication, is momentarily made childlike in her pleasure at the cakes served at a grand hotel: 'row upon row of little freaks, inspirations, little melting dreams'.[10] Cakes play a similar role in 'The Garden Party' (1922), whose dynamics hinge on the moral question of whether a wealthy family should cancel their summer party because a poor neighbour has just been killed.

A picnic with cakes, from a 1920s advertisement.

The protagonist, Laura, is caught in a liminal state between the hypocrisy and cynicism of the adult and the open sensitivities of the child. It is in this context that she and her sister are faced with a pile of cream puffs from Godber's:

> Of course Laura and Jose were far too grown-up to care about such things. All the same, they couldn't help agreeing that the puffs looked very attractive. Very. Cook began arranging them, shaking off the extra icing sugar . . .
>
> 'Have one each, my dears,' said cook in her comfortable voice. 'Yer ma won't know.'
>
> Oh, impossible. Fancy cream puffs so soon after breakfast. The very idea made one shudder. All the same, two minutes later Jose and Laura were licking their fingers with that absorbed inward look that only comes from whipped cream.[11]

To eat the cream puffs – to fully own the desire they evoke – places Laura momentarily back in the morally honest state of childhood. By the end of the novel, having played Lady Bountiful by taking the leftover sandwiches and cakes to the home of the dead workman, she is fully initiated into the moral bankruptcy of her class, her innocent gift for true empathy lost. There are two ways of looking at the cakes. As extravagant whimsies they signal the decadent consumerism of the bourgeois family, at one with the masses of lilies their irresponsible mother has bought on a whim. But in their ephemerality, their evocation of the simpler past ("'Don't they carry one back to all one's parties?" said Laura'), they emblematize the last moments of childhood.

If French cakes are about pleasure and English cakes, except those of childhood, are about denial, the cakes of North

American literature are all about process. Over and over again we encounter scenes of baking. In Louisa M. Alcott's *An Old-Fashioned Girl* (1870), Tom Shaw, expelled from college and at a loose end, trespasses on the kitchen where his sister's friend Polly is giving lessons in cake baking. Allowed into the hallowed, all-female space and invited to beat the cake mixture,

German girls eating birthday cakes, from a 1930s postcard.

Julianne Moore's 1950s housewife presents her husband with his birthday cake in a still from *The Hours* (2002).

he compares himself in imagination to 'Hercules with the distaff', and finds his employment 'pleasant, if not classical'.[12] The simple, rural Polly – the old-fashioned girl of the title – is a counterpoint to the smart sophisticated girls who are the usual social companions of the wealthy Shaw family. Polly's skills as a baker, and the warm welcoming environment she creates in the kitchen, mark her out as precisely the wife Tom needs, and the novel eventually obliges. In Canadian author L. M. Montgomery's *Anne of Green Gables* series (1908 onwards) the baking of cake plays a repeated and significant part in establishing the life of the rural community of Avonlea and the travails of passionate, imaginative orphan Anne as she tries to fit in. In the opening chapter, a neighbour surveys the prepared tea-table in Marilla Cuthbert's house, assessing that company must be expected but, because of the everyday china, crab-apple preserves and only one sort of cake 'it could not be any particular company'.[13] Cake in the novels are an essential part of social relations, carefully graded in number, complexity and luxuriousness so that everyone knows their place. Later in the first novel Anne begs to be allowed to bake a cake in honour of the new minister and his wife. She feels the pressure of the occasion deeply, as she confesses to her bosom friend Diana:

> It's such a responsibility having a minister's family to tea. I never went through such an experience before . . . We're to have two kinds of jelly, red and yellow, and three kinds of cookies, and fruit cake, and Marilla's famous yellow-plum preserves that she keeps especially for ministers, and pound cake and layer cake, and biscuits as aforesaid . . . I just grow cold when I think of my layer cake. Oh, Diana, what if it shouldn't be good! I dreamed last night that I was chased all round by a fearful goblin with a big layer cake for a head.[14]

Anne's cake rises beautifully – 'it came out of the oven as light and feathery as golden foam' – but her triumph is short-lived: 'Mrs Allan took a mouthful of hers and a most peculiar expression crossed her face; not a word did she say, however, but steadily ate away at it.' Anne has flavoured the cake with anodyne liniment instead of vanilla, unable to smell the difference because of a cold. The mix-up and Anne's succeeding shame are played as comic, but the abiding assumption is that a girl should, by the age of eleven, already be a skilled cake-maker, and that much social cachet rests on her abilities. (In another iconic 'orphan' narrative, Eleanor H. Porter's Pollyanna is taught to cook by the members of the Ladies' Aid; since they cannot agree about the correct way to bake bread they begin her culinary education with cakes – she has only got as far as chocolate and fig before she is removed to live with her straight-laced aunt.)[15] Throughout the long series of 'Anne' novels (ten in total, written between 1908 and

1939), cakes continue to function as barometers of social status and as objects of complex exchange. 'I wish I could get Miss Ellen's recipe for pound cake', sighs Aunt Chatty, the gentle wistful widow with whom Anne boards in *Anne of Windy Poplars*, 'She's promised it to me time and again but it never comes. It's an old English family recipe. They're so exclusive about their recipes.' 'In wild, fantastic dreams', reports Anne in her letter to her fiancé Gilbert, 'I see myself compelling Miss Sarah to hand that recipe over to Aunt Chatty on bended knee.'[16] The notion of the secret recipe, as discussed in the previous chapter, is particularly dominant in North American food culture; the idea that this secret recipe is English, passed down in the family for generations, gives it the added cachet of the early immigrant; its withholding is clearly seen by Anne as the act of social aggression that it is.

Cakes are often transformative objects in North American literature. In Eudora Welty's *Delta Wedding* (1945) (a novel in which there are so many cakes that they form a veritable grammar of Southern female traditions), nine-year-old Laura joins her large rumbustious extended family in their plantation home in the Mississippi Delta, in preparation for the wedding of one of her cousins. On her first night, still reeling from the exuberance of the eccentric family, her aunt Ellen invites her to help make a cake. The passage in which the baking of the cake is described is an extraordinary one. We are privy to Ellen's stream of consciousness as she follows the old family recipe, inherited from Mashula, a distant ancestor of her husband's family. She worries about her daughter's upcoming wedding and her brother-in-law's collapsing marriage as she separates and beats the egg whites, creams the butter and sugar, and directs Laura in the making of almond paste and Roxie, her African-American maid, in the grating of coconut. So much is signified in this passage – the matrilineal line of Southern female power; the vexed, complex relations between black and white women, as Ellen and Roxie bicker amicably over whose kitchen it is and who can dismiss who from it; and the importance of cakes in carrying tradition. It is significant that the cake-making is described in such detail that a reader could bake the cake from the directions given. Reader and writer are united in a process of recipe exchange that knits together women and community.[17]

6
Postmodern Cakes

In the 1990s the cake, long-overlooked fuddy-duddy aunty, underwent a radical makeover and emerged – *ta-dah!* – as the cupcake. Previously a stalwart of children's baking lessons and birthday parties, the cupcake was suddenly the acme of glamour.[1] Grand caterers offered them as cocktail nibbles, fashionable weddings had piles of decorated cupcakes instead of a tiered traditional cake, and the queues at New York's famous cupcake bakeries were down the street. How did this happen? We might begin with the Magnolia Bakery, the small kitschy shop in New York that is said to have started the craze, but in fact the story begins in the 1980s, with the revival of interest in traditional modes of baking in both America and Britain. The key figure was almost certainly Martha Stewart. She first came to public attention in 1982 with the publication of *Entertaining*, which combined recipes and party plans with home decorating advice and lifestyle chat, accompanied by lots of pictures of Martha, elegantly dressed-down, in her painstakingly restored early-nineteenth-century farmhouse, surrounded by the antiques she had 'sourced' to fill it. On the back of that first book she built a multimedia empire of magazines, books, TV shows, websites and products of all sorts. Her brand of carefully

Cupcakes as spiders.

laid-back WASP-y chic was combined with an OCD-level attention to detail, which she managed to convey to her fans as a quality to be emulated. Nothing was too much trouble – preparing a banquet for 40 with authentic eighteenth-century ingredients, table settings and lighting; converting your house into a tastefully gothic extravaganza for Hallowe'en, with muslin ghosts, eerily emptied rooms and hundreds of art-carved pumpkins; or baking your own three-tier wedding cake. Although her bossy perfectionism was constantly ripe for parody, Stewart, through the subtle manipulation of fantasies of class, succeeded in transforming the arena of the domestic into something that the educated middle-class woman could allow herself to value. As far as cake is concerned, in taking baking and its history seriously, she offered the perfect riposte to the cake-mix culture: Martha doesn't bake a Betty Crocker layer cake, she tracks down antique hand-carved *speculaas* moulds from Holland, finds the authentic recipe to bake in them, makes hundreds, and themes an art-directed party for scores of neighbours around the cookies. Much like Elizabeth David in the 1960s and '70s, she offers her acolytes a challenge: an almost impossible ideal to live up to. That the halo seems hardly dented by her recent stint in jail for insider trading says much for the Teflon-coated resilience of the brand she has fashioned herself into. Martha's cakes are European-style – *Bûche de Noel* (the rich chocolate Yule log that is the traditional French Christmas cake), *Baba au Rhum*, Italian cornmeal cake, stollen – but she also revives traditional American cakes – Coconut, Devil's Food and the like. She creates a powerful nostalgia for a past of warm, cosy kitchens and the smell of grandma's baking.

It was precisely this fantasy that motivated high-school friends Jennifer Appel and Allysa Torey to set up the Magnolia Bakery in 1996: 'As two women passionate for the culinary and homemaking arts . . . Allysa and I wanted to express our desires and creativity through a business that emphasizes a slow-paced, wholesome way of life reminiscent of 1950s America', wrote Appel in the introduction to the *Magnolia Bakery Cookbook* (1999).[2] The bakery opened in a small corner shop in New York's funky West Village. The interior was decked out from vintage stores and flea markets to resemble grandma's kitchen and the cakes were baked right there in the shop. The cupcakes came about rather by accident – one day they had extra batter left over, and Torey ran out to buy some cupcake papers. They were such a hit that the window was gradually taken over by the seried ranks of the baby cakes. Customers began queuing around the block, and the bakery had to set a limit of twelve cupcakes per person to have a hope of filling the demand. The phenomenon went global in 2000 when the bakery featured in an episode of *Sex and the City*, the hit TV show about single New York women, when Carrie and her girlfriends joined the queue for the buttercream-swirled treats. By then Appel and Torey had gone their separate ways, riven by creative differences.[3] Appel founded a rival bakery, Buttercup, across the street, and soon many more cutely named bakeries (The Little Cupcake Bakeshop; Happy, Happy, Happy; The Polka Dot Cake Studio) popped up all over the city. The appeal of the cupcake is clear: it is small: just enough to satisfy, but not *too* fattening (though actually, its proportion of sugary, buttery topping to cake is such that a slice of cake would probably contain fewer calories). It is portable, ideal for fast-paced city life. But above all it is its cuteness, its candy-coloured evocation of the innocent joys of childhood that draws in the punters.

In Britain Nigella Lawson saw the appeal of the cupcake very clearly and put it at the centre of her second book, *How to Be a Domestic Goddess* (2000): cappuccino cupcakes, carrot cupcakes with cream-cheese icing, burnt-butter brown-sugar cupcakes, chocolate-cherry cupcakes, lavender cupcakes, espresso cupcakes, Coca-Cola cupcakes, banana, cherry and white-chocolate cupcakes – the book is stuffed full of the diminutive mouthfuls, which Lawson champions as the ideal ending for the modern dinner party. Lawson's book, sub-titled *Baking and the Art of Comfort Cooking*, is all about play-ing mother, dressing up in a metaphorical long apron and producing banana bread, Boston cream pie, snickerdoodles and strawberry shortcakes. Producing, in other words, not the baking of the mothers of her British readers, but that of some idealized American mom, a fantasy constructed from the advertising images of the 1950s and '60s, a sepia collage of which adorns the book's endpapers. The book is all about playing mother rather than actually being her – it is notable that the main recipients of the baking are not to be our

Wayne Thiebaud, *Cake Window (Seven Cakes)*, 1970–76, oil on canvas.

Claes Oldenburg, *Floor Cake*, 1962, mixed media.

children, but ourselves. Lawson is well aware of the iconic/
ironic appeal of the cupcake: a single *Ur*-cupcake graces the
book's cover, white icing dripping down the side, top inex-
pertly domed, sugar flower rakishly off-centre, as vulnerable
in its see-through paper case as a young girl in a nightie.

These cakes are postmodern because they are what the
theorist Jean Baudrillard calls simulacra – copies of an original that does not any longer exist, or perhaps never did.[4]
Self-consciously recreating an 'innocent' past that only existed
in films, advertisements and the pages of magazines, these
miniature cakes speak of the *idea* of cake, of a yearning for
childhood, for pastel-coloured reassurance and simple
pleasures, for home, for mother, for the smell of baking,
for being allowed to lick out the mixing bowl. They join the

Cake sculpture: wedding cake made of 2,000 plaster casts of human bones.

many other 'idea cakes' that flesh out our sense of what cake is: the huge iced cakes out of which scantily clad girls jump in golden-age Hollywood films, the factory-perfect ranks of identical iced cakes in the art of Wayne Thiebaud, the enormous cloth cake-sculptures of Claes Oldenburg, repulsive in their great soft oozings. That cake is as much an idea as a reality is suggested by the sheer number of such creations: the thousands of internet pages given up to knitted cakes, crocheted cakes, cakes in clay, in Lego, in basketwork. Representing kitsch and nostalgia, femininity and childhood, manufacture and home craft, tradition and innovation, they speak to us of the many things cake has been and is yet to be.

Recipes

Ancient Cakes

Panforte

Perhaps one of the closest survivals of the compressed cakes of the classical world, this cake is traditionally served at Christmas. It is recorded in thirteenth-century Siena but may well be older. The white pepper in a sweet cake summons up the authentic flavours of the Middle Ages. It contains a small amount of flour, but is otherwise rather closer to nougat than to a modern cake.

Ingredients
180 g hazelnuts
100 g almonds
200 g mixed candied fruits, chopped
1 tsp cocoa powder
¾ tsp ground cinnamon
¼ tsp each of ground allspice, grated nutmeg and ground coriander
⅛ tsp ground white pepper
80 g plain white flour
100 g granulated sugar
125 ml runny honey
icing sugar and ground cinnamon to decorate

Butter a 21.5 cm round cake tin. Line base with parchment paper.

Preheat oven to 150°C. Toast whole nuts in dry pan over gentle heat, stirring frequently, until golden brown. Cool. Mix together fruit, cocoa, spices and flour in large bowl. Stir in cooled nuts. In a small heavy saucepan dissolve the sugar and honey. Bring to the boil and cook rapidly until syrup reaches 130°C or the hard ball stage (when a drop in cold water forms a hard ball). Pour syrup onto dry ingredients and mix rapidly. Press into tin with wet fingers to form a smooth firm layer. Bake for 1 hour. Remove from oven and allow to cool, when it will harden considerably. Dust the top thickly with icing sugar and then lightly with cinnamon. Store in an airtight container at room temperature for up to two weeks. Serve in thin slices. This cake makes a good gift.

Gugelhopf

This recipe has been traced back as far as sixteenth-century Poland, and is popular, under various names, in many parts of northern Europe. It is cooked in a mould with a central funnel, which allows the oven heat to penetrate to the middle of the large cake. I cook mine in a Bundt tin – a design of cake tin famous in America, invented in the early twentieth century in imitation of the Gugelhopf moulds of Europe. Bundt tins come in all sorts of inventive designs (mine is a castle) and are usually used in America for Angel Cake mixtures, where the high proportion of egg whites produces the 'whoosh' necessary to fill the tin. This recipe is based, with adaptations, on that given by Barbara Maher in her excellent *Cake*.

Ingredients
100 ml milk, warmed to hand hot
10 g dried yeast
75 g sugar
300 g strong plain flour
70 g raisins
30 ml Kirsch or brandy

100 g butter
1 whole egg
3 egg yolks
1 tsp salt

Preheat oven to 200°C.

Sprinkle yeast and 1 tsp of flour onto the warm milk. Stir then allow to stand for 10 minutes until foamy and yeasty-smelling. Stir in 60 g of the sifted flour and set aside. Put raisins to soak in brandy or Kirsch. In an electric mixer beat butter and sugar until light coloured and fluffy. Add both whole egg and yolks, alternating with a spoonful of flour. Add yeast mixture and sifted flour and salt. Using a dough hook, beat very well at top speed until the mixture coheres together into a smooth mass and separates from the sides of the bowl. This may take up to 10 minutes on top speed. Drain raisins and shake in a small quantity of flour. Stir into dough. Sprinkle dough with a small amount of flour and leave in a warm place until doubled in size. Grease 23 cm gugelhopf mould or bundt tin with almond oil or melted butter. Knock back risen dough and knead slightly, then coil into base of mould. Leave again to rise until within a few centimetres of top of tin. Bake for about 30 minutes until golden and firm, and when an inserted skewer comes out clean. Turn onto a rack to cool. Dust with icing sugar to serve.

Classic Cakes

Victoria Sandwich

Named in honour of the Queen, who enjoyed the cake at tea in her home on the Isle of Wight, where she spent much of her later years. The original Victoria Sandwich was a classic pound cake mixture, with equal quantities of butter, sugar, flour and eggs. Later versions produce a tenderer crumb with the substitution of cornflour or potato flour for a portion of the flour. Victoria's was sandwiched with jam, but in the twentieth century it became common to add a layer of whipped cream as well.

225 g soft unsalted butter
225 g caster sugar
4 large eggs
1 tsp vanilla extract
200 g self-raising flour
25 g cornflour
¾ tbsp milk

4 tbsp strawberry or raspberry jam
125 ml double cream
Caster or icing sugar to finish

Butter 2 x 21 cm sandwich tins and line the bottoms with circles of baking parchment cut to size. Preheat oven to 180°c. Cream butter and sugar until very pale and fluffy then stir in vanilla. Sieve flour and cornflour together. Add eggs one by one, alternating with spoonfuls of flour if the mixture looks like curdling. Gently fold in the remaining flour. Stir in milk to make a dropping consistency. Divide between the tins, level mixture, and bake for approximately 25 minutes, until the cakes begin to come away from the sides of the tin and a skewer comes out clean. Leave to rest in the tins on racks for a few minutes, then turn out onto racks and gently peel off paper. Leave to cool completely before filling.

Gently whip cream. Place one cake on serving platter, spread with jam and then cream. Place second cake on top. Dust with caster sugar or sieved icing sugar.

Variations

This cake lends itself to an almost infinite variety of different fillings and toppings.

Coffee and Walnut Cake

An old-fashioned Women's Institute-style classic: the only good use for Camp coffee. Stir 125 g chopped walnuts into the cake mixture with the flour. Omit vanilla extract and substitute 2 tbsp Camp coffee essence for 2 tbsp of the milk. Sandwich the finished cakes with a coffee butter cream made by beating 175 g softened butter and 350 g sieved icing sugar until white and creamy, then stirring in 1 tbsp coffee essence (or more to taste). Spread over top and sides. Decorate with walnut halves.

Light Chocolate Cake

Substitute 50 g cocoa powder for flour in the cake mixture. Make chocolate buttercream as for coffee but substitute 1 rounded tbsp cocoa for the coffee essence. When butter, sugar and cocoa are creamed together, add one tbsp hot water to slacken.

Cupcakes

This mixture is ideal for cupcakes, which can be flavoured and decorated in a huge variety of ways. Place muffin or cupcake cases in muffin or cupcake tins. Fill half-full with mixture. Bake for 10–15 minutes until well risen and golden. Decorate with a simple water icing (icing sugar, coloured and flavoured with a few drops each of food colouring and flavouring extracts then thinned to dropping consistency with cold water) or a swirl of buttercream. For the full childhood-relieved experience, top with sprinkles or dolly mixtures.

Boiled Fruit Cake

This recipe came from a friend of my mother's, so we always knew it as 'Jane Glover's Fruit Cake'; it is one of my father's favourite cakes. The method produces a rich-tasting cake from fairly frugal ingredients: boiling the fruits with the sugar and butter causes them to swell into plump succulence. This cake keeps well and is delicious spread with butter or eaten to accompany a strong cheese in the tradition of northern England.

Ingredients
345 g mixed fruit
115 g butter
115 g sugar
150 ml water
1 beaten egg
230 g self-raising flour

Put fruit, sugar, butter and water into a saucepan. Cook gently, stirring periodically, until butter is melted and sugar is dissolved. Simmer slowly for twenty minutes until fruit is round and nearly bursting and remaining liquid is thick. Allow to cool until you can comfortably place your hand on the side of the pan. Add beaten egg. Stir in flour. Turn into a greased 1.25 litre loaf tin. Bake in a moderate oven 150°–180°c for 1¼ – 1½ hours until shrunk away slightly from sides of pan and a skewer inserted in the centre comes out clean. Cover the surface of the cake with greaseproof paper if necessary to prevent it getting too brown. Cool in the tin for 10 minutes before turning out onto a rack.

Lemon Drizzle Cake

One of the most popular British cakes. At cake and school fetes these unassuming little loaf cakes are invariably the fastest to sell. My version is what we might call a double-drizzle: the warm cake is soaked in the sharp lemon syrup and left to cool, then it is drizzled again with a simple lemon icing.

Ingredients
100g butter

100g caster sugar
2 large eggs
100 g plain flour
½ tsp baking powder
zest of 1 lemon
2 tbsp warm water

For syrup:
juice of 1 lemon
50 g granulated sugar

For icing:
100 g icing sugar
juice of 1 lemon
2 tsp lemon zest (optional)

Preheat oven to 180°C. Beat butter and caster sugar until pale and fluffy. Sift flour and baking powder. Mix the eggs gradually into the butter mixture, alternating with spoonfuls of flour if the mixture threatens to split or curdle. Fold in the remaining flour. Stir in lemon zest and water. Turn into a greased 1.25 litre loaf tin, and bake for up to 1 hour. Test the cake with a skewer when it begins to shrink away from the sides of the tin.

While it is baking, melt the granulated sugar gently with the lemon juice to form a syrup, taking care not to let the mixture get too hot. Remove cake from oven, leave in the tin, and prick it all over with a skewer. Pour lemon syrup slowly over the cake, allowing time for it to be absorbed. Set cake on rack in its tin and allow to cool.

Meanwhile, prepare icing. Gradually add lemon juice to icing sugar until a smooth pouring consistency is achieved. Be prepared to adjust amounts of sugar or juice if icing is too thin or too thick. Add lemon zest if desired. When cake is cold, turn out of the tin and slowly pour the lemon icing over the top, allowing it to drizzle down the sides.

Hazelnut and Raspberry Cake

I have made this cake for many years, and it never fails to please. A German-style cake, which substitutes ground nuts for flour, this is delightfully squidgy, and satisfying without being cloying. It works very well as a dessert for a party.

6 large eggs
180 g caster sugar
220 g whole hazelnuts

250 ml double cream, whipped
150–200 g raspberries

Grease and flour a 24 cm springform tin. Line base with a circle of baking parchment.

Place nuts in a dry frying pan (preferably a heavy-bottomed cast iron) and toast carefully over a low heat, shaking pan to rotate them. This can also be done in a moderate oven, but the nuts must be checked frequently as they burn very easily. When golden in patches allow to cool. Grind the cooled nuts in a food processor. The aim is to reduce most of the nuts to a coarse flour but retain some larger chunks for texture. Be careful not to process too far or they will release their oils and turn to nut-butter. Separate the eggs carefully. Whisk yolks and sugar until pale, creamy and very thick. Stir in nuts. Whisk egg whites to firm peaks then gently fold them into the yolk mixture with a large metal spoon. Turn into tin and bake until cake begins to shrink away from sides of the tin – approximately 45 minutes. Leave in tin to cool for 10 minutes, then release clip and turn out onto rack. When completely cold, carefully cut cake in half horizontally, then fill with whipped cream and raspberries.

If preferred, the mixture can be baked in two layers in shallower cake tins, in which case the layers will take about 25–30 minutes to bake.

Unusual Cakes

French Savoury Cake with Artichokes, Olives and Gruyere

This is my adaptation of one of Sophie Dudemaine's recipes. It produces a dense texture – halfway between cake and a sourdough bread. It is good served with a salad, or the way the French most typically eat it: cut into small squares as an aperitif.

Ingredients
3 eggs
150 g plain flour
2 tsp baking powder
100 ml sunflower oil
125 ml whole milk
100 g grated gruyere
250 g bottled artichoke hearts (drained weight)
50 g green olives stuffed with peppers
pinch of salt and pepper

Drain the artichoke hearts. Puree half, roughly chop the remainder. Roughly chop the olives. Put flour, baking powder, and eggs in a food processor and process until smooth. Add the grated gruyere. With motor running add first oil then egg in a thin stream. Add artichoke puree and briefly process again. Scrape three quarters of the mixture into a greased loaf tin. Scatter over most of olives and chopped artichokes. Add rest of mixture and top with remaining artichokes and olives. Cover and leave to rest for at least an hour: the resting time produces a lighter cake. Bake in an oven preheated to 220°C for 30–35 minutes or until well risen, golden and firm. Allow to cool before removing from tin.

Tres Leches Cake

This Latin American pudding cake is extremely rich: a very light fat-free sponge soaked with more than its own weight in creamy milk mixture. It is classically served topped with sweetened vanilla-flavoured whipped cream or with a caramel sauce, but I prefer it plain and accompanied by fruit – berries work well. You may find that you are left with a small quantity of sauce that the cake will not absorb. This can be served alongside the cake as it is, or boiled to reduce it to a thick toffee sauce. The cake must be kept in the fridge because of the milk content; this recipe makes 8–10 generous portions.

Ingredients
Cake:
4 large eggs, separated
115 g caster sugar
115 g plain flour
1 rounded tsp baking powder
Scant ½ tsp cream of tartar

Soaking cream:
395 ml sweetened condensed milk
250 ml evaporated milk
250 ml double cream
1 tsp vanilla essence
2 tbsp brandy (optional)

Preheat oven to 175°c. Grease and flour a 24 cm springform cake tin. Beat egg whites to soft peak stage, then add half of the sugar and beat again to stiff peaks. In another bowl whisk yolks and remaining sugar until pale yellow. Sift the flour and raising agents. Gently fold egg white mixture and flour alternately into yolk mixture. Pour into pan. Bake for 15–20 minutes until just golden; a skewer or toothpick should come out clean. Cool on wire rack in cake tin.

Whisk all liquids together. Place cake (still in its tin) on a tray or plate with side to catch any liquid which escapes. Prick cake thoroughly all over with a skewer. Slowly pour over about a third of the soaking cream and wait for it to be absorbed. Continue to pour the cream over in batches, pricking more holes in the cake if necessary. Let stand in the fridge for at least thirty minutes, or until it absorbs cream. Remove sides of pan before serving.

References

Introduction

1 Value Added Tax: the sales tax levied on luxury items in the UK. All cakes are counted as staple foods and zero rated, as are plain biscuits. 'Luxury' biscuits, which includes any covered with chocolate, are liable for the tax.

1 Cakes through History

1 John M. Wilkins and Shaun Hill, *Food in the Ancient World* (Oxford, 2006), pp. 128–9.
2 Ibid., p. 127.
3 Dorothy Hartley, *Food in England* [1954] (London, 1996), pp. 634–5.
4 C. Anne Wilson, *Food and Drink in Britain from the Stone Age to the 19th Century* [1991] (Chicago, IL, 2003), pp. 247.
5 Ibid., p. 264.
6 Ibid. p. 234.
7 'Cake, n.', *Oxford English Dictionary*, 1a.
8 Geoffrey Chaucer, *The Canterbury Tales* [c. 1400], General Prologue, l. 668; a buckler was a round medieval shield.
9 Shakespeare, *Twelfth Night* [1623], II, iii, 115.
10 John Strype, ed., *Stow's Survey of London* [1598] (London, 1720), vol. II, p. 441.

11 Gervase Markham, *The English Huswife* [1615], repr. as *The English Housewife*, ed. Michael R. Best (Kingston, Ontario, 1986), pp. 97–8.

12 Sir Kenelm Digby, *The Closet of the Eminently Learned Sir Kenelm Digby Knight Opened* [1669], p. 267.

13 Hannah Glasse, *The Art of Cookery Made Plain and Easy* (London, 1747), p. 138.

14 Barbara Maher, *Cakes* (Harmondsworth, 1982), p. 162.

2 Cakes around the World

1 Jean Paul Sartre, 'Nourritures', *Verve*, IV (1938), pp. 115–16.

2 See Anne Willan, *Great Cooks and Their Recipes: From Taillevent to Escoffier* (London, 1995), pp. 57–9. She notes that the very different style of *Le Patissier* and *Le Cuisine françois* casts some doubt on the later attribution of the former to La Varenne, concluding that if he did write the book, he must have done so in close association with an Italian pastry cook.

3 *Larousse Gastronomique* (London, 2001), p. 885.

4 Elizabeth David, *French Provincial Cooking* (London, 1960), p. 434.

5 Rick Rodgers, *Kaffeehaus* (New York, 2002), p. xi.

6 Claudia Roden, *A New Book of Middle Eastern Food* (Harmondsworth, 1986), p. 485; *The Book of Jewish Food* (London, 1997), p. 514.

7 Laurens van der Post, *African Cooking* (New York, 1971), pp. 162; 164.

8 In 1958 just over 23 per cent of the cakes consumed by the Japanese were of Western style; by 1989 the figure was nearly 54 per cent. (See Andrew Gordon, ed., *Postwar Japan as History* (Berkeley, CA, 1993).

9 See Laura Mason, 'Sachertorte', in *The Oxford Companion to Food*, ed. Alan Davidson, and Rodgers, *Kaffeehaus*, pp. 60–61.

10 'Answers to Queries', *Ladies' Home Journal* (August 1889), p. 19. Food historians have been unable to agree on any likely source of the 'Lady Baltimore' name.

3 The Culture of Baking Cake

1 Gervase Markham, *The English Huswife* [1615], repr. as *The English Housewife*, ed. Michael R. Best (Kingston, Ontario, 1986), p. 64.

2 John Earle, *Micro-cosmographie* [1628], quoted in John Dover Wilson, *Life in Shakespeare's England* (Cambridge, 1911), p. 226.

3 Josephine Terry, 'No Trouble Tea Fancies', *Food Without Fuss* (London, 1944), p. 55.

4 Philip and Mary Hyman, 'France' in *The Oxford Companion to Food*, ed. Alan Davidson (Oxford, 1999).

5 Jillian, our French au pair, assures me that in his family rabbit cake is a favourite.

6 Sophie Dudemaine, *Les Cakes de Sophie* (Geneva, 2000). Sophie also gives recipes for sweet cakes – banana, *marron glacé*, coffee with chocolate and whisky – but these seem to be less popular.

7 See Laura Ingalls Wilder, *Little House on the Prairie* (1935), *These Happy Golden Years* (1943).

8 Irma Rombauer, *The Joy of Cooking* [1936] (London, 1943), p. 573.

9 Myrna Johnston, *Better Homes and Gardens* [1953], quoted in Laura Shapiro, *Something from the Oven: Reinventing Dinner in 1950s America* (New York, 2004).

10 For a fuller discussion of these issues see Susan Marks, *Finding Betty Crocker: The Secret Life of America's First Lady of Food* (New York, 2005) and Laura Shapiro's excellent *Something from the Oven*. In Barbara Kingsolver's *The Poisonwood Bible* (1998), the characters take packets of Betty Crocker cake mix with them on a trek into the jungle.

4 The Rituals and Symbolism of Cake

1 Tamra Andrews, *Nectar and Ambrosia: An Encyclopedia of Food in World Mythology* (Santa Barbara, CA, 2000), pp. 52–4.

2 Henry Teonge, *The Diary*, ed. G. E. Mainwaring (London,

1927), p. 120; cited in Bridget Ann Henisch, *Cakes and Characters: An English Christmas Tradition* (London, 1984), p. 50.

3 Mary Douglas, 'Food as an Art Form', *The Active Voice* (London, 1982), p. 105.

4 See Simon R. Charsley's excellent *Wedding Cakes and Cultural History* (London, 1992).

5 At the moment of writing, American wedding organizers are just beginning to offer fake cakes on the Japanese model to their own customers.

6 This most famous and perplexing of cake-sayings dates from the sixteenth century (it is recorded in John Heywood's *Proverbs and Epigrams* of 1562) and originally took the more logical form of 'You can't eat your cake and have it'.

5 Literary Cakes

1 Marcel Proust, *A La Recherche du temps perdu*, trans. as *Remembrance of Things Past*, vol. 1: *Swann's Way; Within a Budding Grove* by C. K. Scott Moncrieff and Terence Kilmartin (New York, 1957), pp. 48–51.

2 Charles Dickens, *Great Expectations* [1860–61] (Harmondsworth, 1965), p. 113.

3 Proust, *A La Recherche*, vol. III, p. 110.

4 Ibid., vol. IV, pp. 283–4.

5 Colette, *Claudine s'en va*, trans. Antonia White as *Claudine and Annie*, in *The Complete Claudine* (New York, 2001), p. 523.

6 Gustave Flaubert, *Madame Bovary* [1857], trans. Geoffrey Wall (Harmondsworth, 2003), p. 27.

7 Jane Austen, *Emma* [1815] (Oxford, 1944), p. 19.

8 Elizabeth Gaskell, *Cranford* [1853] (Harmondsworth, 1986), p. 111.

9 Lewis Carroll, *Alice's Adventures in Wonderland* [1865] (London, 1968), p. 18.

10 Katherine Mansfield, 'The Young Girl' [1922], *The Collected Stories of Katherine Mansfield* (Harmondsworth, 1945), p. 298.

11 Katherine Mansfield, 'The Garden Party' [1922], *The*

Collected Stories of Katherine Mansfield, p. 252.

12 Louisa M. Alcott, *An Old-Fashioned Girl* (London, 1870), p. 276.

13 L. M. Montgomery, *Anne of Green Gables* [1908] (Harmondsworth, 1977), p. 10.

14 Ibid., pp. 145–7.

15 Eleanor H. Porter, *Pollyanna* [1913] (Harmondsworth, 2003), p. 50.

16 L. M. Montgomery, *Anne of Windy Poplars* (published in England as *Anne of Windy Willows*) [1936] (Harmondsworth, 1994), p. 30.

17 See Ann Romines's article 'On Eudora Welty's Cake', available at http://gwenglish.blogspot.com/2007/04/ann-romines-on-eudora-weltys-cakes.html, accessed 29 July 2009.

6 Postmodern Cakes

1 The term 'cupcake', confusingly, has two separate etymologies, both dating from the nineteenth century. It refers, particularly in America, to cake ingredients measured using cups, but it also, increasingly, comes to refer to cake mixture baked in small cups or tins. By the twentieth century this was the dominant meaning and the tins began to be supplemented by commercially produced 'muffin' or 'cupcake' papers.

2 Jennifer Appel and Allysa Torey, *The Magnolia Bakery Cookbook: Old-Fashioned Recipes from New York's Sweetest Bakery* (New York, 1999), p. 9.

3 Torey wanted to stay true to their original vision of a small, quirky neighbourhood bakery; Appel, more business-savvy, wanted to follow the money.

4 'Simulation is no longer that of a territory, a referential being or a substance. It is the generation by models of a real without origin or reality: a hyperreal.' Jean Baudrillard, 'Simulacra and Simulations', *Jean Baudrillard, Selected Writings*, ed. Mark Poster (Stanford, CA, 1988), pp. 166–84.

Select Bibliography

Beranbaum, Rose Levy, *The Cake Bible* (New York, 1988)

Charsley, Simon R., *Wedding Cakes and Cultural History* (London, 1992)

David, Elizabeth, *English Bread and Yeast Cookery* (London, 1979)

Dickie, John, *Delizia!: The Epic History of the Italians and their Food* (New York, 2008)

Henisch, Barbara Ann, *Cakes and Characters: An English Christmas Tradition* (London, 1984)

Maher, Barbara, *Cakes* (Harmondsworth, 1982)

Mennell, Stephen, *All Manners of Food: Eating and Taste in England and France from the Middle Ages to the Present*, revd edn (Chicago, IL, 1996)

Ojakangas, Beatrice, *The Great Scandinavian Baking Book* (Minneapolis, MN, 1999)

Rodgers, Rick, *Kaffeehaus* (New York, 2002)

Shapiro, Laura, *Something from the Oven: Reinventing Dinner in 1950s America* (New York, 2004)

Spencer, Colin, *British Food: An Extraordinary Thousand Years of History* (London, 2002)

Willan, Anne, *Great Cooks and Their Recipes: From Taillevent to Escoffier* (London, 1995)

Wilson, C. Anne, *Food and Drink in Britain from the Stone Age to the 19th Century*, revd edn (Chicago, IL, 2003)

Websites and Associations

Cake Shops and Designers

Charm City Cakes
www.charmcitycakes.com

Peggy Porschen
www.peggyporschen.com

Jane Asher
www.janeasher.co.uk

Konditor and Cook
www.konditorandcook.com

Ottolenghi
www.ottolenghi.co.uk

Betty's Tea Rooms
www.bettys.co.uk

Cake Recipes

The Joy of Baking
www.joyofbaking.com

Martha Stewart
www.marthastewart.com

Nigella Lawson
www.nigella.com

Baking Mad
www.bakingmad.com

Cake Baker
www.cakebaker.co.uk

Cake Enthusiasts

A Nice Cup of Tea and a Sit Down
www.nicecupofteaandasitdown.com

Cake Wrecks
http://cakewrecks.blogspot.com

Cupcakes take the Cake
http://cupcakestakethecake.blogspot.com

Real Baking with Rose Levy Beranbaum
www.realbakingwithrose.com

Bakerella
www.bakerella.com

Smitten Kitchen
http://smittenkitchen.com

Acknowledgements

Roehampton University provided research leave in 2007 which allowed me to begin work on this book. The students in my BA and MA 'Literature of Food' seminars gave me much food for thought on the nature and importance of cake, and colleagues including Cathy Wells-Cole, Sarah Turvey, Jenny Hartley, Kate Teltscher, Laura Peters and Simon Edwards were, as always, supportive and interested. I am particularly grateful to Susan Matthews for first pointing me in the direction of French savoury cake. I would like to thank Paula Thompson, Pat O'Toole, Caroline Elliot, Johanna Dickin, Judith Murray, Ciarán O'Meara, Tara Lamont, Frances Wilson, Sarah Moss, Simon Larter, Nicola Ansell, Victoria Stewart, Mary Grover, Kathy Farquharson and Louise Lee for their enthusiastic interest and suggestions. Tracy Anderson was extremely generous with her art-historical expertise. The librarians at Leeds University's Brotherton Library and the British Library were very helpful. I would also like to thank Michael Leaman and Andrew Smith of Reaktion Books for their advice, and Martha Jay and Harry Gilonis for their expert work preparing the book for publication. Many thanks to my parents Pat and Brian Humble for supplying some of the recipes. Elletra Conci and Jillian Chazalette provided much needed help and support on the domestic front as well as very interesting information about Italian and French cakes respectively. As always, I owe a huge debt to my husband Martin Priestman and my son Luke, who were helpful and enthusiastic about the project, despite the fact that they don't much like cake.

Photo Acknowledgements

The author and publishers wish to express their thanks to the below sources of illustrative material and/or permission to reproduce it. Locations, etc., of some items not included in the captions for reasons of space are also given below.

Photo akg-images, London: p. 104; photo akg-images, London/ ullstein bild: p. 47; photo Associated Newspapers/Daily Mail/Rex Features: p. 80; Bodleian Library, University of Oxford: p. 15; The British Museum, London (photos © The Trustees of the British Museum): pp. 11, 12 (Department of Greek & Roman Antiquities), 38, 57, 59, 61, 77 (Department of Prints and Drawings); from Marie-Antoine Carême, *Le Patissier Pittoresque* (Paris, 1842): p. 33; from Lewis Carroll, *Alice through the Looking-Glass* (London, 1872): p. 100; photo Design Pics Inc/Rex Features: p. 110; photo Everett Collection/Rex Features: p. 91; The Fitzwilliam Museum, Cambridge: p. 84; Galleria d'Arte Moderna di Milano: p. 31; photo Harris & Ewing, Inc./Library of Congress, Washington, DC (Prints and Photographs Division - Harris & Ewing Collection): p. 85; Photo Carol Howard: p. 18; Kunsthistorisches Museum, Vienna: p. 74; photo Michael Leaman/Reaktion Books: p. 45; photos Library of Congress, Washington, DC (Prints and Photographs Division): pp. 35, 69 (James Guthrie Harbord Collection), 51; Metropolitan Museum of Art, New York: p. 54; Musée Fabre, Montpellier: p. 75; Museum of Modern Art, New York: p. 114; photo © oleg66// 2010 iStock International Inc.: p. 6; courtesy the Oldenburg van

Index

italic numbers refer to illustrations; **bold** to recipes